W9-AZZ-392

TO THE NINES

A practical guide to horse and rider turnout
for dressage, eventing and hunter/jumper shows

JENNIFER CHONG

Alpine
PUBLICATIONS
Loveland, Colorado

Upper School Library
Glenelg Country School
12793 Folly Quarter Road
Ellicott City, MD 21042

To the Nines
Copyright ©2006 by Jennifer Chong.
All rights reserved. No part of this book may be used or reproduced in any
manner whatsoever, including electronic media, internet, or newsletters,
without written permission from the publisher, except in the case of brief
quotations embodied in critical reviews. For permission, write to Alpine
Publications, Inc., P.O. Box 7027, Loveland, CO 80537.

ISBN 1-57779-064-2

Library of Congress Cataloging-in-Publication Data

Chong, Jennfier, 1978-
    To the nines : a practical guide to horse and rider turnout for dressage,
    eventing, and hunter/jumper shows / by Jennifer Chong.
        p. cm.
    ISBN 1-57779-064-2
    1. Show riding. 2. Dressage. 3. Eventing (Horsemanship) 4. Hunter trials
    (Horsemanship) I. Title.

    SF295.2.C56 2004
    798.2--dc22
                                                         2004050276

The information contained in this book is complete and accurate to the
best of our knowledge. All recommendations are made without guarantee
on the part of the author or Alpine Publications, Inc. The author and publisher disclaim any liability with the use of this information.

For the sake of simplicity, the terms "he" and "she" are sometimes used to
identify an animal or person. These are used in the generic sense only. No
discrimination of any kind is intended toward either sex.

Many manufacturers secure trademark rights for their products. When
Alpine Publications is aware of a trademark claim, we identify the product
name by using initial capital letters.

Cover Design and Layout: Laura Newport
Font Cover Photo: Carien Schippers
Back Cover Photo: Deborah Ravinsky
Editing: Deborah Helmers
Photographs: by the author unless otherwise indicated.
Illustrations: Jennifer Chong

1 2 3 4 5 6 7 8 9 0

Printed in the United States of America.

For the horses in my life,
past, present, and future.
They are my daily inspiration.

TABLE OF CONTENTS

Acknowledgments vi
Introduction vii

The Rider 1
Selection of Attire 2
  Schooling Apparel...2
  Hats and Helmets 3
  Competition Attire 5
Finishing Off the Look...25
  A Stick-y Situation: Artificial Aids.........................25
  Boots..27
  Jewelry 34
  Hair...35
Keeping the Look Fresh 40
  Keeping Clean 40
  Keeping Cool...43
  Ladies Only 47
  Barn Clothes...49

The Horse..51
Your Spick-and-Span Horse 52
  Grooming...52
  Methods of Restraint 56
  Bathing..59
Troubleshooting and Spot Cleaning................................64
  Hooves 64
  White Markings 65
  Clipping 67
  Coat Problems 67
  Sheath and Udders..69
  Chesnuts...71
  Show Ring Shine 71
Coat and Mane Treatments 73

Trimming 73
Mane Pulling 75
Braiding...77
Clipping 92
Don't Bug Me! Dealing With Insects 99

The Tack 103

Selection of Equipment 104
Quality 104
Style 106
Buying Used Tack...............................118
Care of Tack 119
Why Care for Tack?.............................119
Everyday Cleaning 121
Special Occasion Tack Care 123
Complete Cleaning and Conditioning 124
Agh! It's Alive: Neglected Tack 130
Tack Storage 131
Tack Repair, or "My Hero, the Shoe Repair Guy" 131

The Show 133

Prepare to Compete 134
The Paper Chase 134
Chef D'Equipe 142
Labeling 146
The Traveling Horse 150
Stall and Barn Setup...........................154
Studs 168
Countdown! 169
Ice and Poultice Treatments...................172
Laundry..173
Final Words 178
Helpful Lists..............................179
Competition Checklists 173

Other Sources of Information 186
About the Author 195

ACKNOWLEDGMENTS

I would like to acknowledge (in no particular order) the following people, all of whom had an influence on me that was vital in the realization of this book:

The mentors and trainers who have shaped me both as a rider and as a horseman, including Christiane Noelting, Judy Klus, Sheila McKell, Rose Von der Leyen, Bill and Lori Hoos, Reinhard and Hannes Baumgart, Christine Scarlett, and now Gerhard Politz; special thanks also to barn managers and friends Robin Connor and Terri Dougherty.

Julia Wendell and Barrett Warner for allowing me to use their lovely An Otherwise Perfect Farm for the photos; the other riders at the farm who put up with me scurrying around with my camera, borrowing equipment, begging them to model for me, particularly Jennifer Tanio and Christine Hohmann; and also Anne Kincaid for letting me do a makeover on Tally.

Deborah Ravinsky, for being a fantastic sounding board and for contributing some great photos, especially the ones from Rolex.

Julia Wendell (again!) for her insightful and thoughtful comments on an early draft of the manuscript.

My college roomate, Kim Schulze, for having tolerated me cleaning tack, polishing boots, and hanging soggy horse laundry in our kitchen, living room, and front porch for two years so I'd have something to write about.

My parents, Fay and Edie Chong, for their support in this harebrained endeavor.

Dr. Ruth Hodges, for encouraging me at every juncture.

Jeremy Ecke, for his faith in me.

James Lin and Linda Schlossberg, for their invaluable guidance and advice.

And, of course, Betty McKinney, my publisher, who believed in the project and who enabled me to fulfill my lifelong dream of becoming an author.

INTRODUCTION

There always seem to be a million things to do to get a horse and rider ready for a competition. How to manage it all and still arrive on time, in one piece, looking good, and physically and mentally ready to go? I am from a non-horsey family. Since age ten, it has been my own my responsibility to figure out all the details of preparing myself and my horse for competition. Gradually I learned and refined a set of strategies and techniques to make everything come together, but this took me years of competing and grooming for myself and others at events, at hunter/jumper and dressage shows, and at Pony Club ratings and rallies, not to mention the hours and hours as a working student at event and dressage barns in the United States and Europe. From my wonderful first horse Amelia, a dark bay Appaloosa, through Romi, my Westfalen, to Steel, my Thoroughbred, to Donovan, my young Hanoverian, to Juilliard, my Bavarian warm blood, I have continued to seek new ways to make my preparation faster, easier, and more effective. And then I thought, "Hey, other people are going through this too! Why not write down all the secrets and tricks of the trade I've developed and discovered and share my hard work?" A book like this would have been a great aid to me along the way—I hope you will find it helpful in your own competitive equestrian journey. Have fun!

Jennifer Chong
August 2005

Final tack adjustments (Rolex Kentucky CCI**** Three Day Event). Photo by Deborah Ravinsky.

THE RIDER

Selection of Attire • Finishing Off the Look • Keeping the Look Fresh

SELECTION OF ATTIRE

SCHOOLING APPAREL

For schooling at home, you have a free rein in choosing what you want to wear. Many riders wear pants—jeans are a popular choice—and full or half chaps. (Here's this book's first cool tip: Rubbing a bar of soap along the length of the zipper on new chaps will cause it to slide more easily.) Others prefer to school in boots and breeches. Many riders have separate helmets and boots for schooling so as not to get their nice ones scuffed up from day-to-day wear and tear. If you want to wear your helmet for both schooling and shows, you can use a helmet cover. (Lycra helmet covers serve this purpose well, although if you have the option of using a helmet cover for competition (for example, for cross-country), satin or nylon ones are more appropriate.) If you are taking a lesson, make sure that you are dressed in such a way that your instructor can see your position: wear clothes that are reasonably form-fitting, and tuck in your shirt. A lesson is not the time for a big billowy poncho. Clean and polished boots present a tidy, professional appearance that shows that you respect your instructor's time and knowledge and that you are serious about learning.

For riding in a clinic or an informal schooling show, forego the chaps and vented schooling helmets. Instead, wear conservatively colored breeches, polished boots, a belt if your

Schooling attire.

breeches have belt loops, and a collared shirt such as a polo shirt, with your velvet helmet or hunt cap. Your neat appearance will make a good first impression on the clinician and spectators.

HATS AND HELMETS

I am a strong advocate of wearing protective headgear at all times while mounted on any horse for any activity. Although most of us know helmets are a good idea, many riders tend to get a little casual about wearing them, thinking, "I only need one if I'm jumping," "My horse is so quiet," or "It's too hot for a helmet today." But we usually need our helmet when we least expect it. My worst horse-related accident happened not while jumping or galloping or starting a green horse, but while I was on Amelia, my wonderful, bombproof first horse, trotting in a dressage arena. She hit a patch of footing that looked fine but was slippery under the surface, and we both went down. I landed on my head and was taken by ambulance to the emergency room and then to Intensive Care for what turned out to be a concussion. Thank goodness I was wearing my helmet—it may have saved my life, and it definitely saved me from a more severe head injury. As it is, I have no memory of the accident; when I finally came to in the middle of the night in the hospital, nine hours of my memory had been wiped out, including several hours before the fall. Friends had to fill me in on what happened.

Some helmets are labeled "Hat Notice and Warning: Item of Apparel Only" and others, "ASTM F-1163-00/SEI Certified." Although they may have chinstraps and feel hard-shelled, the "item of apparel only" helmets are not likely to protect your head in a fall. ASTM/SEI helmets are designed and rigorously tested to self-destruct upon sufficient impact so that they will absorb the shock

Clinic attire.

Approved helmets: GPA 'Euro hat' or 'skunk hat' and Troxel Legacy schooling helmet.

More approved helmets: jockey helmet with nylon cover and Troxel Grand Prix Gold velvet helmet.

of a crash instead of allowing your brain to slam into your skull. They will need to be replaced if you've fallen on your head wearing one, but most ASTM/SEI manufacturers offer a generous replacement policy in such cases. You send the helmet back to the manufacturer, and they check it for structural integrity (you can't tell with the naked eye whether or not the helmet is damaged). Then they either fix the helmet or send you a new one, either for free or at a very nominal price.

Some barns' insurance policies require all riders to wear ASTM/SEI helmets. They are also required for all juniors when mounted and all adults when jumping at recognized hunter/jumper shows. As of 2003, they were required for the jumping phases of events as well. Due in part to these new rules, the designs of many of the current helmets are now better looking and better fitting than the ASTM/SEI helmets of a few years ago. My personal favorite for competing is the Troxel Grand Prix Gold velvet show helmet, and I school in a vented Troxel Legacy or GPA Titanium, which are cooler. Even if not required to wear an ASTM/SEI hat, consider wearing one anyway not only for your own safety, but also to set a good example for others.

COMPETITION ATTIRE

In choosing your competition attire, my advice is the same as I will later give you regarding tack: Buy high quality items that are classic enough in style to be useful year after year. Even if you are watching your budget, you can afford to bow to trends in smaller items such as shirts, gloves, and breeches. If you are a still-growing kid or teenager, you will be able to go a little more trendy since you'll probably outgrow the stuff before it falls out of fashion.

The United States Equestrian Federation (USEF, formerly AHSA) rule book provides rules for what is allowable to wear in each discipline, but it is really no good as practical advice. What is legal according to the rules has little relation to what is actually acceptable according to the tradition of the individual sport and to its current fashions; tweed coats, for example, are within the rules in dressage, but no one has worn them in the dressage ring in the United States for years. What follows is a guideline of items of apparel that will probably always be appropriate in their respective sports, along with some current trends, tips, and recommendations.

DRESSAGE

Stock Ties
Although I didn't have this option at Pony Club competitions (where riders who wear stock ties must use the conventional and

untied sort), I much prefer to ride in a stock tie bib, also called a dickey. Since it looks so much better if you tie it yourself, I use an untied (instead of pre-tied) stock tie bib with Velcro at the back. I tie it at home or in the trailer in front of a mirror and pin it, then take it off and leave it until I need it. Thus I avoid a last-minute scramble to get my stock tie tied perfectly—it is already tied to my satisfaction and all I have to do is Velcro it on at the neck and secure it around the waist and I'm ready to go. Be sure to buy the kind

THE TIMELESS LOOK

- Black velvet helmet or hunt cap (a top hat is okay if you're really, really good; derbies are also legal but are less common) through fourth level, top hat for FEI

- Black or dark blue dressage coat (four buttons down the front and cut longer than a hunt coat) through fourth level, black or dark blue (midnight blue) shadbelly for FEI; canary vest or vest points with shadbelly

- White shirt

- White stock tie with a horizontal plain gold stock tie pin

- White gloves (black gloves are also okay at the lower levels, but white is more common)

- White breeches (preferably full seat)

- Black or dark brown belt (if the breeches have belt loops)

- Black dressage boots (dress boots are also okay; field boots are allowed but if you plan to show in dressage frequently, get dress or dressage boots)

Dressage or show jumping attire.

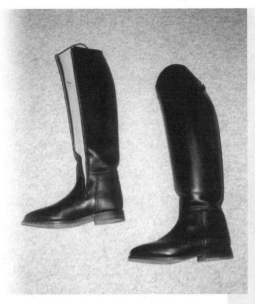

Extra stiff dressage boots with zippers.

RECENT TRENDS

- Dark blue coat with cream breeches, often seen with cream shirt, stock tie, gloves, and saddle-pad. This color scheme looks especially nice with brown tack.

- High waisted breeches (often beltless)— these tend to flatter the figure and look especially good under shadbellies

- Velvet lapels, with or without gold or silver piping

- Dark blue top hat or hunt cap (to match coat)

- Washable coat

- Super-stiff dressage boots with square toes, zippers up the inside of the leg, and Spanish tops (higher on the outside than the inside)

TIPS

with Velcro at the neck, though; without Velcro or snaps or something, you can't tie it beforehand, defeating the whole purpose. I also like stock tie bibs because when the weather is hot enough to be very uncomfortable but not hot enough for coats to be waived, I can wear a stock tie bib over a sports bra with my coat on top and eliminate the extra shirt layer. This does mean, however, that I must warm up with my coat on!

Stock Ties Part Deux

When I went to Lexington, Kentucky for the USPC National Championships for dressage in 1995, I was the only one on my five-member team who knew how to tie a stock tie. So all week I tied stock ties not only for myself, but for my three other riding team members (the stable manager doesn't ride). On the last day of competition, there was a stock-tying competition between the thirty-four teams. The horse management judges let us choose whether to enter the "poofy" or "crisp" division. I tied my teammate Christy's stock tie, and won the poofy division! So if you want to learn "crisp" go elsewhere, but to learn "poofy," follow this guide:

Step 1. *Drape the stock tie around your neck.*

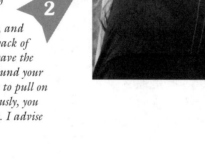

Step 2. *Stick the long end through the loop or slot in the stock tie, and bring it around the back of your neck. You now have the stock tie wrapped around your neck, and if you were to pull on both ends simultaneously, you would soon turn blue. I advise against this.*

Step 4. *Grasp an end in hand, the left end in your left, the right end in your right.*

Step 5. *Cross the right end over the left end. There is now a triangular "hole" formed by the right end, the left end, and your chest.*

Step 3. *Alternately tug on the ends until they are even. They should now hang vertically down your front.*

Step 6. *Pull the right end through the triangle. (Steps 5 and 6 are the same as the first step of tying shoelaces.)*

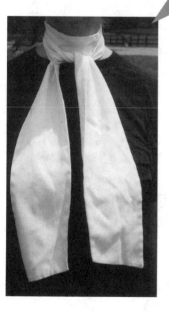

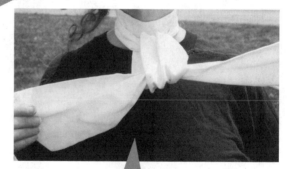

Step 7. *Now cross the new left end over the new right end. Pull the new left end through the triangular hole. You have now tied a square knot.*

Step 8. *Tighten and adjust the stock tie so that it is tight but not uncomfortably so and the knot is centered under your chin. Do not pull the knot tight; it should be poofy.*

Step 9. *Pull the ends of the stock tie up behind the knot and over it. The ends should now hide the knot and hang down your front.*

Step 10. *Cross the ends and fluff the top part that's over the knot so it looks tidy and symmetrical, not lopsided.*
Step 11. *Using a plain gold stock pin, horizontally pin through the top part (through both ends and the knot). Make sure the pin is straight.*

Step 12. *Secure the tails of the ends with normal safety pins. These will be hidden under your coat and will keep the tails from flying out of the coat and flapping around while you're riding.*

Gloves

White gloves have got to be the most impractical item of clothing we wear in dressage. One ride and they are no longer white! For this reason, I always choose washable white gloves instead of the conventional leather kind. I like the cotton ones with rubber pebbles all over the palms and fingers for grip. They are ridiculously inexpensive, and you can throw them in the wash. If you Velcro them to the belt loops of your show breeches, they won't get lost in the laundry and they'll be there when you need them at your next show. They don't last forever, but by the time they are looking a little ragged, it is likely that they also are not as bright white as they once were. These gloves are so economical that you probably won't balk at replacing them. Retired show gloves can always enjoy a second life as part of your schooling wardrobe, too!

Breeches

Except for my coat, I don't buy any riding clothes that I have to dry clean. All my breeches are required to go in the wash. Suede full seats seem to do fine, but leather full seats will get stiff and scratchy over time, making them very uncomfortable to ride in. To remedy this, simply turn your breeches inside out and rub a thin layer of Carr & Day & Martin Leather Balsam (or Passier Lederbalsam or another such conditioner) on the inside of the leather. This is the flesh side and it will absorb better. Hang the breeches up and allow the leather to air dry indoors for several days. You can then wear them. They will be much softer and suppler, but if they are too sticky for your liking, you can wash them before wearing. At first, the leather seat on the outside will have darker and lighter colored spots due to differing amounts of conditioner, but the discoloration will even out with wear. You will probably not need to repeat this process very often—perhaps once every year or two, depending on how much the breeches are worn and washed.

Top Hats and Derbies

Although the rulebook says that competitors may wear protective headgear at any level without penalty, it is more appropriate for upper level competitors to wear top hats. If you are very good it is okay to wear a top hat at the lower levels (from a style standpoint; helmets, of course, are safer). I see no reason for derbies. They are not that flattering nor are they fashionable in the United States (although they are worn frequently in Europe); you might as well have the extra protection of a helmet if you are not going to wear a top hat. Other than the absence of any protection whatsoever for the head (the most serious drawback), the big problem with top hats and derbies is keeping them in place. A helmet is kept in place by its harness. A hunt cap usually will just stay on. But top hats and derbies are more precarious. If you wear your hair in a bun for competitions, you can help steady your top hat/derby with a simple method. Sew a very, very thin string of elastic into the lining of your headgear so that one end is above your left ear and the other above your right ear. The length of elastic should pass around the back of your head, under your bun. This will stabilize your hat a bit, but it won't be enough if a big gust of wind hits you from the front. Another trick is to stitch or stick the hook part of Velcro (the stiff plastic part, not the fuzzy part) around the inside of your hat so that it Velcros onto your hair and hairnet. (Note: Your hair will look rather funky when you take the hat off!) If your hat is tight, this Velcro arrangement could be uncomfortable, but it will help the hat stay in place. On a really windy day, though, the best advice is to leave your top hat or

Top hat and protective carrying case.

derby in the barn and wear a helmet—you will have enough to think about without wondering just when your hat is planning to go flying through the air and just where it will decide to land.

Horse and rider ready to show jump (Rolex Kentucky CCI**** Three Day Event).
Photo by Deborah Ravinsky.

EVENTING: DRESSAGE PHASE

THE TIMELESS LOOK

- Black velvet helmet or hunt cap with a short coat; a top hat with a shadbelly (only for three-day events or advanced horse trials)

- Black or dark blue dressage coat (four buttons down the front and cut longer than a hunt coat) for horse trials through intermediate and three-day events through the two star level, black or dark blue (midnight blue) shadbelly for three-day events (any level) or advanced horse trials

- White shirt

- White stock tie with a horizontal plain gold stock tie pin

- Black gloves—white are also acceptable but rarely seen at events except with shadbellies (I usually wear white anyway)

- Beige breeches—white may also be worn but is less common than beige; fewer people wear full seat breeches than in a dressage show

- Black or dark brown belt (if the breeches have belt loops)

- Black boots—dress, field, dressage, or hunting (with brown tops) are all acceptable, although field boots are most common

RECENT TRENDS

Darker, greenish-beige breeches (Tailored Sportsman or imitations) as seen in the hunter world

Dressage Clothing

You may dress for the dressage phase of an event just as if you were competing at a dressage show, or you may choose to follow the conventions specific to eventing.

Stock Ties

See Dressage for stock tie selection tips.

Hunter Clothing

TIPS

It is also acceptable (although less common) to go into the dressage phase of an event in hunter-style attire. As a matter of fact, you could do this at a dressage show as well and nobody would kick you out. If you show chiefly in the hunter-jumper world with just an occasional foray into eventing or dressage, by all means wear your hunter attire. But if your focus is more on dressage and/or eventing, it is best to choose clothes that are more mainstream in these sports.

Fourth level dressage. Photo by Jody Ciliberto.

EVENTING: CROSS-COUNTRY

Helmet Rubber Band

Because there is no brim to anchor the helmet cover in place, helmet covers on jockey-style helmets are prone to slipping or coming off entirely during your cross-country go. Bit of Britain sells a great solution very inexpensively: a large rubber band that goes over the cover to hold it firmly in place. You have plenty to worry about while you're going around cross-country—you don't need to worry about losing your helmet cover too!

THE TIMELESS LOOK

- Jockey-style helmet (e.g., International Euro Eventer, Charles Owen Pro Skull Cap, Lexington Trac Star) with satin or nylon (not lycra) helmet cover

- Cross-country vest (Tipperary vests are preferred)

- Polo shirt, long-sleeved shirt, or sweater, depending on the weather

- Gloves

- Beige or white breeches

- Boots—dress, field, hunt, black, brown

- Cross-country watch

- Medical armband

Cross-country attire.

RECENT TRENDS

You can have a little fun in designing your cross-country attire. Many people choose one or two colors as a theme and coordinate their vest, helmet cover, and shirt to match. You can also take that a little further and wear colored gloves and breeches, and put a matching saddlepad on your horse. But when you also coordinate your horse's galloping boots, browband, and two-toned petal bell boots you have, in my opinion, crossed the line of good taste! Color coordinate, but be understated.

Medical Armband

If you have just begun eventing in the past couple of years, remembering to wear your medical armband for the jumping phases may not be much of a problem. But if you are one of us dinosaurs from the pre-medical armband era (1997 and earlier), you may tend to forget this new rule. You will not be allowed to compete in either jumping phase, nor will you be allowed to warm up for these phases, without a complete, up-to-date medical armband of the correct color (the USEA changes the color of the medical card every year or so). To make myself remember mine, I plant it in a strategic place the day before. Some of my favorite locations are:

- Looped through my belt
- Stuck in my helmet
- Hooked to my cross-country vest
- Attached to the girth for my jumping saddle

If you stick your armband in any of these places, it will be very difficult to forget, because you'll see it as you're getting ready. I guarantee you, you won't forget your girth for cross-country, so you'll be sure to remember that armband. And if you do forget to put it on your arm before you head out, it will be there anyway, dangling from your belt or smushed in your helmet. (Far better than having to gallop back to the trailer or barn to find it when you're running late anyway!)

TIPS

Pinnies

It is really distracting to have your pinny come untied and start flying around while you're warming up or on course. Prevent this from happening by securing it well before you get on. Put the pinny on over your vest and thread the strings from the back of your pinny through the lacing at the sides of your vest to stabilize it. Tie each set of strings with a square knot (right over left, left over right) or, better yet, a surgeon's knot (right over left twice, then left over right) and then tie into a bow. Tie the loops of the bow together (like double knotting a shoelace). Your pinny will be a pain to take off, but it won't come untied while you're riding either!

If you have more than one horse to ride cross-country, first put on the pinny with the number of your last horse. On top of that, put the second to last horse, and so on. That way when you've finished each cross-country run, you can simply remove the top pinny and you're ready to go for the next one—no arriving at the start box with the wrong number, no last minute scramble because you can't find your next pinny.

Extra Security

Cross-country is an extreme sport. And you usually can't win if you fall off. To give yourself a little extra grip, wrap Vetrap around the tread of your stirrups. You can coordinate with your cross-country colors if you wish, but black would never be inappropriate. There are also special stirrup pads which offer extra grip (e.g., Sure

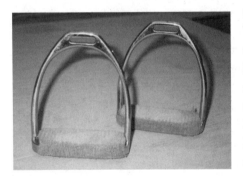

Grip pads), but you may also want to smear your saddle with Sadl-Tite, a grippy substance that comes on a stick and will help you keep from slipping. After your ride, use castile soap or another cleanser to get rid of the Sadl-Tite. Bienenwachs Lederpflege-Crème leather balsam (in the orange tub) also works well, with the added advantage that you won't need to remove it when you're done. It will also condition and waterproof your leather to some degree, although I still prefer Passier Lederbalsam and Carr & Day & Martin as conditioners. Full seat breeches will also give you a little more purchase on your saddle.

Vetrap on stirrups for security.

Watches

Get a good cross-country watch, no matter what. I used to go cross-country just with my everyday wristwatch, but the buttons are impossible to work when you've got bulky gloves on, and the little numbers are hard to see when you're galloping on course. I finally broke down and started watch shopping, and after looking at several models I picked the Optimum Time watch (or, as it's better known, "the big yellow watch"). It's expensive but well worth it, because it is easy to use even with gloves, easy to read even while galloping, and was designed specifically for cross-country. You can set it to count down to zero from your optimum time so a glance at your watch will tell you how many minutes or seconds you have left before you begin to accrue time penalties. Once it's hit optimum time (or whatever you set it at) it will beep distinctively and start to count up. The setting I like best counts up from zero and beeps every minute. If you walk your course with a meter wheel and find your minute markers (every 520 meters for 520 mpm, every 450 meters for 450 mpm, etc.), the beeping every minute will really help you gauge your pace. You can buy the Optimum Time watch from Bit of Britain or any eventing-oriented tack shop worth its salt.

Clean, conditioned tack is safe tack, whether trail riding at home or on the cross country course (Rolex Kentucky CCI**** Three Day Event). Photo by Deborah Ravinsky.

EVENTING: STADIUM JUMPING PHASE

Stadium/dressage coat

One coat can do double duty as a stadium and dressage coat. If you never show in pure dressage at all, you may want to go with a slightly shorter coat than you would if you were a pure dressage rider, since it is a bit easier to jump in a shorter coat. There is more movement involved in jumping than in dressage, so the coat will need to be a tad roomier or have some give in the shoulders and arms. The RJ Eventer coat from Bit of Britain is a good choice. If you do compete in dressage shows, you will probably want to choose a coat that is appropriately styled for dressage but that allows you enough freedom so that you can jump without

RECENT TRENDS

It is perfectly fine to turn out for the stadium jumping phase of eventing as you would for a hunter/jumper show. If you also compete in the hunters or jumpers, you may prefer this option.

THE TIMELESS LOOK

- Jockey style helmet with black nylon or satin cover (not lycra), GPA style helmet, or black velvet helmet (navy helmets and helmet covers are also permissible; until recently all helmet covers were allowed and many people used their cross-country helmet covers for stadium)

- Black or dark blue coat (your dressage coat is okay)

- White shirt

- White stock tie with a horizontal plain gold stock tie pin

- Gloves—style is a matter of personal preference; some forego gloves for this phase

- White or beige breeches (may be full seat)

- Black or dark brown belt

- Black boots—field, dress, or hunt boots w/ brown tops

- Medical armband

bursting at the seams or getting tangled up in your coattails. My Pikeur Diana has worked well for me.

Medical Armband

Again, as recommended for cross-country, it is a good idea to plant your medical armband in an obvious place so you won't forget it.

TIPS

Nearing the last fence in show jumping—always a good feeling! (Rolex Kentucky CCI**** Three Day Event). Photo by Deborah Ravinsky.

HUNTERS

THE TIMELESS LOOK

- Velvet hunt cap or velvet helmet (helmets meeting ASTM/SEI safety standards are required for juniors), top hats with shadbellies
- Dark, conservatively colored (e.g. navy, black, or charcoal), three-button coat with or without pinstripes (or hunter-style shadbelly for hunter classics)
- Light-colored shirt (ratcatcher) with matching choker
- Small pin or monogram on choker
- Beige breeches (or jodhpurs for children in paddock or jodhpur boots) (knee patches only—no full seats allowed!)
- Black leather gloves
- Brown belt
- Black boots (dress or field) or brown jodhpur or paddock boots for children
- Garter straps for children wearing jodhpurs and short boots

RECENT TRENDS

Styles change more rapidly in the hunter ring than they do in the worlds of dressage and eventing, which is fun for the fashion savvy but difficult for those of us with a limited budget. Here are a few of the recent looks:

- Light-colored coats, such as tan, gray, or olive, often plaid
- Darker, bolder-colored shirts, including blues and greens
- Monogram on choker
- Tailored Sportsman breeches in greenish beige (be careful—these are dry clean only!)
- Field boots with swagger tabs and punched toe caps
- Beat-up, weathered-looking velvet hunt caps
- GPA style helmets, especially for juniors (see *Jumpers*, below)

Hunter or show jumping attire.

Numbers

To tie your number on your back, use shoelaces (black or some color to blend in with your hunt coat) instead of yarn or safety pins. Safety pins look tacky, and yarn is cumbersome and less sturdy. Find a slender, dress shoe-type shoelace (not the fat, soft kind on sneakers) that's long enough to go around you and tie in the front, or tie two together and put the knot behind the number. For flat classes where the judge may want you to move your number to the inside each time you change direction, it will be easier if you use a single shoelace so you don't have to maneuver around the knot. For best results when you tie the shoelace, thread one end through the middle buttonhole on your coat and wrap the other end once around the middle button. This will keep your number from riding up or sagging.

TIPS

Children

Although it is becoming increasingly common to see young children in tall boots, it is always appropriate for pony and (young) children's division riders to compete in the hunter ring in paddock or jodhpur boots, garters, and jodhpur pants (this also goes for jumpers, eventing, and dressage). Tall boots are expensive and children grow quickly, so jodhpurs are a far more practical and economical approach for parents to take when choosing show clothes.

Photo © Jody Ciliberto.

JUMPERS

RECENT TRENDS

After years of scorning helmets in favor of hunt caps which do little in case of a fall, many jumper riders are now embracing a new breed of ASTM/SEI certified safety helmets, sometimes referred to as "skunk hats" or "Euro hats." These helmets have a distinctive metallic center stripe that goes from the center of the front of the hat to the center of the top, and they are covered with a soft, suede-like material or sometimes velvet. Although these safer helmets are not at all traditional looking, they are currently very popular and even make appearances in the hunter ring at the big shows now, particularly in the junior and amateur divisions.

Jumper attire is also becoming more casual. Even at the big shows, in many weekday or lower level jumper classes you will find competitors in a polo shirt, breeches, boots, and hat instead of the full coat and dress shirt ensemble. If you plan to "dress down," ask the show management or the steward to make sure that it is appropriate to do so for the class, day, and show you have in mind. Always have your traditional attire with you just in case, however.

You also see people going into the jumper ring in hunter attire, which is completely appropriate, and even sensible and convenient, since many people show in both divisions.

Rider well turned out for the hunter ring (Devon Horse Show).

THE TIMELESS LOOK

- Black velvet hunt cap or helmet
- Black or dark blue three-button coat
- White or light-colored shirt
- Choker (monogram or pin) or stock tie (pin)
- Black or brown belt
- White breeches (usually knee patch)
- Gloves of choice (or none at all)
- Black boots (field or dress)

FINISHING OFF THE LOOK

A STICK-Y SITUATION: ARTIFICIAL AIDS

RULES

In many cases you will want to wear spurs or carry a stick, whip, crop, or bat. Before entering the ring or leaving the startbox, remember to check the rules as to what is allowed and what isn't. For example, at dressage shows you may wear rowel spurs in any test and carry a whip in most tests (except at championships, FEI sanctioned competitions, and a few others, so check!). However, you are never allowed to wear rowel spurs in your dressage test at an event, and you will be eliminated if you do so. Check also the allowed dimensions: You could face elimination for riding with a whip or spurs that are longer than allowed.

WHIPS

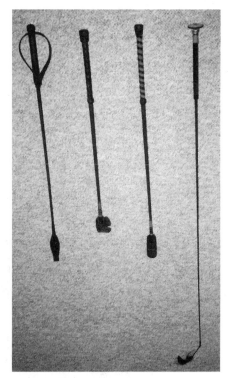

Most dressage riders carry a black dressage whip if they choose to use one. Event riders in both jumping phases favor jockey style bats, or they may choose a traditional crop for the show jumping phase. If a hunter rider carries anything, it should be a black or dark brown crop, but double-check to make sure it is appropriate

From left: dressage whip, jumping bats, crop.

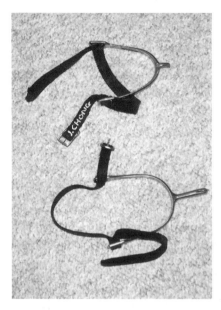

Spurs of different lengths: short Prince of Wales spurs and longer rowel spurs.

to carry anything at all in your class. Jumper riders use jockey style bats or crops.

SPURS

Spurs are worn so that the rider can sharpen and refine the leg aids. Effective use of spurs requires the leg position to be steady enough so that the rider doesn't inadvertently jab or pester the horse, which could make him anxious or dull to the leg aids. If you wear spurs, make sure they are legal for your discipline (if you are competing) and appropriate for the horse you are riding. Short to medium length, plain, blunt-ended Prince of Wales spurs, worn with the shanks pointing down, are usually fine in most situations for most horses that require spurs. If your horse is so sensitive that short Prince of Wales spurs bother him, he probably reacts well enough to your leg aids that you don't need spurs anyway. If you are required to wear them in competition (they are required for FEI dressage tests and intermediate and above eventing dressage tests), find spurs with the smallest shank possible. For horses that are prone to get rubs or spur marks (in which the hair is rubbed away under the spur), I

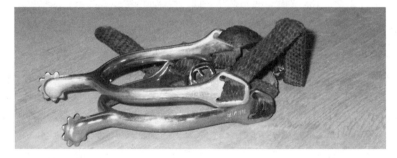

Sunburst rowel spurs.

prefer rowel spurs; when used judiciously, rowels will roll gently across the horse instead of scraping like plain spurs do. Many horses tend to get rubbed by spurs when they're clipped in the winter, and thin-skinned Thoroughbreds will get rubs year round. Unfortunately, some thin-skinned horses may become ticklish and "goosey" with rowel spurs, in which case the spurs become distracting to the horse and thereby useless as an aid.

Dressage riders probably have the most leeway in terms of the type of spurs they can wear. Most riders choose smooth or "sunburst" rowels, or the plain, blunt-ended ones that are appropriate in the other disciplines. Polish your spurs as you would your stirrup irons. If you use leather spur straps, you should clean and condition them as you would your tack, and you can touch them up with black leather dye or shoe polish if they start to lose their color. Permanent black markers also do the job. I prefer nylon spur straps because they give you a more precise fit: instead of only being able to adjust your spurs to punched holes, you can fasten nylon spur straps anywhere in the weave of the strap. Also, because you wear them on your feet and they often encounter more than their share of mud and water, leather spur straps are likely to dry up and crack unless you are vigilant about caring for them. Nylon spur straps are sturdier. To clean nylon straps, wet a toothbrush and rub it over a bar of castile soap. Dunk your spur straps in water and scrub with the toothbrush, then dunk again. Dry in a well-ventilated place so the straps don't mildew.

BOOTS

If your boots are sparkling clean and shiny, your turnout automatically looks better. I am going to share with you my adaptation of a two page, step-by-step boot shining tutorial that was handed to me long ago at a Pony Club meeting. I have added a few steps, but on the whole the original instructions are quite good (I still refer to that Xeroxed sheet), so I have left the original wording intact as much as possible. Such an involved method of boot polishing may seem intimidating or time-consuming at first, but if you do your boots this way you will have to polish them much less frequently than before and they'll look better than ever. I polish my dressage boots only every third show or so and I could probably go even longer. In between tests I clean them off with castile soap and spiff them up with Blitzglanz (a fantastic instant-shine, siliconed sponge available from tack stores and catalogs) and that's all they need.

HOW TO SHINE DIRTY BOOTS

Items Needed
1. Clean, small sponge
2. Castile soap
3. Bucket of clean water (you will change this periodically)
4. Several clean, soft rags
5. Black leather dye
6. Black wax shoe polish (NOT black shoe cream)
7. Neutral cream shoe polish
8. Old toothbrushes and Q-tips
9. Large, good quality shoe brush
10. Black heel and sole edge dressing
11. Nylon pantyhose or stockings
12. Blitzglanz (or similar instant-shine, siliconed sponge)

You can find all this "shoe stuff" (leather dye, wax shoe polish, shoe cream, and heel and edge dressing, buffing brush, etc.) from the shoe-shining section in a supermarket (usually with cleaning supplies or sundries). You can also buy these items at the tack store or from your trusty shoe repair guy, but they may be more expensive. The greatest place to buy soft rags is, of course, your auto parts store.

Method

1. Use the sponge and plenty of water to take off all dirt and mud. Use the toothbrush to scrub the crevice around the sole and the bottom of the sole itself.

2. After all the mud and dirt are washed off, clean the boots with the sponge and castile soap lather. Wipe all lather off with a clean damp sponge. Use castile soap on a toothbrush to clean crevice around the sole. Allow boots to dry thoroughly.

3. If necessary, when boots are dry touch up the wear mark on the calf area and toe scuffs with black leather dye. Let the dye dry thoroughly for several hours or overnight.

4. Using a clean, soft cloth, rub in black wax shoe polish thoroughly, starting at the top and working down through the shoe. Use enough wax to thoroughly coat the leather, but not so much that the surface becomes gummy. The most important thing is to rub the wax thoroughly into the leather and spread it to a thin film. With a toothbrush or Q-tip, work a bit of wax into the crevice between the sole and the upper. DO NOT put black wax on the inside of the calf—your saddle, saddle pad, and horse will turn black! Let the wax dry for a few minutes.

5. Take a small, clean cloth, dip it in cold water, and wring it out. Rub this damp cloth over the entire boot, starting at the top. The purpose is to harden the wax film on the boot so it will not come off on the polishing brush. Give the boot a couple of minutes to dry.

6. Buff the boots vigorously with the shoe polishing brush. (Always keep separate brushes for black and brown polish. Never mix them, because the brushes will transfer wax of the wrong

color.) Start at the top of the boot with your left arm in the boot. Use long, quick, vigorous strokes until the wax begins to shine. Work over the whole boot until all the wax has been buffed to a high shine.

7. Repeat steps 4, 5, and 6, keeping the black wax off the inner calf. You can repeat this three or four times, adding more thin layers of wax, wiping with the damp cloth, and buffing to a shine. The more coats you add, the higher the gloss you will get, the more protection you give to the leather, and the longer the shine will last. Each time after you wear the boots, gently wipe off dust and dirt, buff lightly with the shoe brush*, and you can keep the boots looking nice for quite a while even if you wear them daily—perhaps till the next competition when you will want a new super-shine. If you only wear the boots in competition, you can probably go a couple shows before redoing them.

*Alternately, wipe off with a little castile and a damp sponge, and apply Blitzglanz once dry.

8. After the final polishing with the black wax, use a small clean cloth to apply the neutral cream polish to the calf area of the boot where it contacts the saddle. This will keep you from rubbing the black boot polish off onto your saddle. Apply plenty of cream polish, rub it into the leather thoroughly, and buff with the black shoe brush. Repeat as necessary until you have a good shine and a good protective coat on the boot.

9. Wad the pantyhose into a ball, then stretch one layer of pantyhose over the ball. Scrub the boots all over, starting from the top, with the pantyhose. This will bring an even better shine to them. Rub the Blitzglanz sponge all over the boots for maximum shine.

10. After the boots are thoroughly shined, apply the black heel and edge dressing to the edge of the sole and heel. Let this dressing dry for several hours before using the boots.

BREAKING IN NEW BOOTS

If you have new boots, the best way to break them in is to ride in them. Make sure they are completely broken in before you go to a show, or you may be setting yourself up for a miserable time. Even if you usually school in chaps or half chaps, you should school in your new boots long enough to get them broken in. How long depends on the type of leather: softer or thinner leather will break in more quickly than stiffer or thicker leather. I would allow ten to fifteen rides at a minimum, no matter how soft the leather.

Most boots, dressage boots in particular, should fit very high on the leg, at least as high as your kneecap and sometimes even higher on the outside. This creates a problem for the break-in period: boots will "drop" about an inch and a half, more or less depending on style and quality, but until they do, they will be an inch and a half too tall! If you walk around with your boots on before they are broken in, they will bend behind the knee, which is very uncomfortable for the back of your knee, never mind the unsightly crease that the boots will soon develop. To solve this dilemma, buy a pair of heel risers to insert into the foot of the boot. These will keep the back of the boot from squashing under your knee because they essentially elongate your calf. Once your boots are sufficiently broken down, you can remove them. It is best to only ride (no walking!) in your boots until they have dropped. Also avoid jumping or galloping or any other activity that would require you to use short stirrups until your boots have dropped. Cranking up your stirrups will cause the back of the boot to squash as well because there will be more bend in your knee. Until your boots are somewhat broken in, try to just use them for flatwork.

If, after your boots have dropped, they are still stiff and uncomfortable in the foot, try wearing them around the house. Put big socks over the feet if you're concerned about scuffing floors, and walk around in them all the time. But for the reasons mentioned above, make sure they have already dropped at least somewhat. If your feet are getting blistered, buy Dr. Scholl's moleskin and put it over the affected areas. You can also work the boots in your hands, bending and flexing them along the creases and folds that developed naturally from your riding and walking.

LET'S GET IT ON!

The easiest way to get boots on and off is with a zipper. If you ride dressage, consider buying boots with zippers on the inside of the calf or having them put in (Euro-American Saddlery does a good job), because then you will skirt the whole boot hook/boot jack issue entirely. Although some field boots are now available with zippers down the back seam, zippers aren't as common for other disciplines.

Make sure your boots aren't too tight when you buy them.

If they become too tight, take them to your shoe repair shop and have them stretched for a few days. Adjust the width of your boot trees accordingly to hold this stretch. You can spray the boots with a product such as Fiebings Boot Stretch, and shake baby powder in them or wear nylon stockings so that they'll slide on better. If that's not enough, go back to your shoe guy and have him put a small elastic insert on the inside at the top. That may be enough to facilitate getting them on and off. If it isn't, it may be time for new boots.

Keep your boot hooks and boot jack where you can find them.

I usually keep them in my boots when I'm traveling. Tie the boot hooks together with a length of baling twine, and hang them on a hook. That way you'll be less likely to lose one.

Have a Plan B.

Two hoof picks (the plain metal kind, not the plastic ones with brushes on the other side) work well as boot hooks in a pinch.

Make sure you keep hoof picks around in your grooming box for such emergencies. (Hoof picks can also make good screwdrivers.) For removing your boots, a helper will work just as well as, and sometimes better than, a boot jack. Sit down on something sturdy so you can hang on without getting dragged out of your seat. Have your helper stand in front of you, back to you, and lean over from the waist. Place one foot between your helper's knees. He should grab the boot around your heel. Put your other foot on the helper's derriere. Push that foot against his bottom while he pulls at the boot he's holding. The combined leverage should make it easy to extricate you from your boot!

BOOT TREES

It is best to keep your boot trees in your boots at all times to promote air circulation and to preserve their shape. You can buy boot trees or you can make them as follows:

TO THE NINES BOOT TREES

Two 1.5-liter water bottles or 2-liter soda bottles, depending on boot size
Newspaper or sheet cotton
Duct tape
Two nylon stockings
Fabric (optional)
Two tennis balls

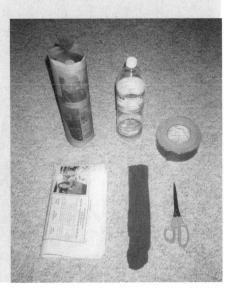

Roll the sheet cotton or newspaper around the bottles until they fit snugly in your boots. Tape the cotton or newspaper closed. Pull a stocking over each covered bottle, over the top of the cotton or newspaper and tie it shut. If desired, sew a fabric cover for each tree. Put one tennis ball in each foot of the boot, and put the tree in the leg.

JEWELRY

Pony Club traditionally has not allowed jewelry for safety reasons. Jewelry can easily catch on something and cause problems or, in the event of a fall, result in more serious injuries. Metal, fortunately, will break under stress; items such as friendship bracelets or necklaces made of embroidery thread generally will not, and so these are worse. Rings will give you blisters. Even something as benign as a small stud earring can cause problems. At a horse management judges' conference, a speaker told of a girl who had had a fall and was apparently fine but then subsequently noticed loss of hearing in one ear. Examination of the area showed a small puncture wound from the stud earring, which caused the hearing impairment. In addition to safety concerns, jewelry looks messy while you are riding. Flying necklaces and swinging earrings detract from your overall turnout.

If you absolutely must wear jewelry while you ride, make it inconspicuous. Tuck your necklace inside your shirt and hope it stays. Get rid of rings, and either take bracelets off or tuck them away under your cuffs or gloves. The only jewelry visible, if any, should be earrings. These should be tasteful, understated, conservative stud earrings (pearls, diamonds, gold or silver balls, or something of that nature).

Some jewelry is easy to remove, but what about jewelry that isn't? Body piercing is becoming more popular, and taking the jewelry out may not always be a viable option—if the pierces are recent, they will close up, and in some locations such as the tongue they'll close even if they were done a while ago. If you do have a tongue ring, keep your mouth closed while competing so as not to distract the judge from your performance. For a pierced nose, wear a nose ring that is small and unobtrusive. The same goes for an eyebrow ring. I knew someone who routinely put a Band-Aid over her eyebrow ring for dressage shows; this may be a good choice, since riding is a rather traditional, conservative sport and many judges may doubt the appropriateness of such things in competition. Nose rings and eyebrow rings can be a safety risk for riders as well, which should be taken into consideration when choosing to have them done. Navel rings and other body piercings are not as problematic since they are under your clothes, which means they are not distracting, nor will they cause a safety problem by catching on something.

HAIR

My hair is currently rather long—it's about waist length. For a while I had it very short, and I have had it at every length in between.

For safety reasons, Pony Club forbade the use of metal pins and clips (they could pierce your head easily in a fall), so I am accustomed to doing all lengths of my hair without bobby pins or barrettes. If you feel compelled to use them, that is your choice, but they're not really needed and can be quite uncomfortable under your hat.

The crucial factor is that your hair be out of the way and inconspicuous—no wisps, no bits sticking out, and if it's in a bun, no bouncing around. This goes for both men and women. All you long-haired guys out there, you'd better invest in some hairnets and elastic bands.

Hair styling equipment: brush, comb, scrunchies, elastics, sturdy hairnet.

FOR HUNTERS

There is but one appropriate way to fix your hair for hunters, so I would recommend that your hair be about shoulder length, though you can still use this style with longer or shorter depending on its thickness. Of course, if your hair is really short you're exempt. Brush your hair, then pull it into a ponytail at the base of your neck so that the hair partially covers your ears (yes, that is part of "the look"). Lean over and fold the pony tail up over your head, pull a hairnet over all your hair, including your bangs, and put your hat on (while still leaning over) to hold the whole production in place. The disadvantage of this arrangement is that you must leave the hat on or the hair won't stay, even if you've pinned it up. But it is the classic style for the hunter ring, and you may import it to the jumper ring if you so desire.

Over-the-ear hunter hair style.

There are two exceptions to this rule: With the new GPA-style hats, juniors may ride with a tiny ponytail (which can only be achieved if the hair is shorter than shoulder-length). Children may go into the pony ring in two pigtails tied with bows. But once these young women have outgrown the ponies (or even before), they should change to the styles above.

FOR OTHER DISCIPLINES

Very Short Hair

A hairnet may help to keep bangs out of your face, but most likely even that isn't needed. Consider yourself lucky, and put your hat on and go.

Slightly Longer Hair

If you can pull your hair into a teeny, tiny ponytail at the base of your neck, do so and enclose everything in a hairnet, including the mini ponytail. If your hair is too short to make a single ponytail, just put the hairnet directly over the hair. You will have a little hair out of the back of your helmet, but it will not be a big deal because it will be contained by the hairnet.

Shoulder-Length Hair

Put your hair in a ponytail and fold it up over your head. Lean over, capture all your hair in a hairnet, and put your hat on. As with the hunter style, you will have to redo your hair every time you put on or take off your helmet. Currently en vogue in the dressage ring is a bun at the base of your neck, tied with a conservatively colored scrunchie. See long hair instructions.

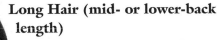

Long Hair (mid- or lower-back length)

Put your hair up in a bun at the nape of your neck, if it will stay, and cover it with a hairnet. A good way to do this is to make a ponytail with one elastic band, and then a bun with a second elastic band. Wrap one hairnet several times around just the bun. Then use a second hairnet to cover your whole head and the bun. You can top this off with a scrunchie wrapped around the

Folded up pony tail (for shoulder-length hair). bun to look like today's international dressage divas. If your hair won't stay in a traditional bun (mine is too slippery and full, other hair is too fine, no matter what kind of hardware you put in), braid it and tie it off at the end with an elastic band. Roll the braid up into a bun and wrap the bun in an elastic band. Cover your head with a hairnet, then twist it once and put the bun in the resulting pouch. Twisting the bun part of the hairnet makes the entire arrangement much more secure. Put another elastic band over the hairnetted bun so it will stay in place. Add a scrunchie if desired. It is important to make sure your bun is low enough so that you can put your hat on, but high and tight enough so that it won't bounce as you ride.

Extremely Long Hair (hip length, knee length, or beyond)

I have never had hair this long, but I have seen the solutions of several who have. Braid it and let the braid hang down your back. Your coat will cover the braid, and since you won't be able to use a hairnet, tuck wisps of hair into your hat as best you can or pin them to keep them secure. If your hair is so long that the braid would stick out the end of your coat or you would sit on it, wind the end of the braid around your belt, making sure you allow enough slack in the braid so you can move comfortably.

Bun with scrunchie.

HAIRNETS

The thin hairnets available at supermarkets and drugstores will actually do you no good. They will tear within a wearing or two, and they won't keep your hair in line. Buy the thicker, sturdier hairnets available from tack stores or catalogs such as Dover or State Line. You can usually find these hairnets in catalogs near the hats and helmets, and you can get them to match your hair color.

ELASTIC BANDS

For elastic bands, the thin supermarket variety will work just fine. Try to get ones that match or blend with your hair color, and always have plenty of extras on hand.

A WORD ABOUT "SHOW BOWS" (SNOODS)

A snood, more commonly known in horsey circles as a "show bow," is a large metal barrette with a hairnet pouch attached and a bow on top. You clip your hair in the barrette at the base of your neck and stuff your hair in the net pouch. Pony Club does not allow these (a sharp metal edge at the back of your head would do you no good in a fall). If you feel compelled to wear one, get one that is quiet and conservatively styled and that will fit all your hair. This means that the net part should be neither too big nor too small: too small and strands of hair will escape and make you look unkempt; too big and the bow will look superfluous. Snoods are impossible to use with conventional hairnets, so you will tend to have the problem of escaping wisps of hair floating around your face.

KEEPING THE LOOK FRESH

KEEPING CLEAN

You've arrived at the show with all your competition attire clean and ready to go. But you still have a few more hours until your first ride, and then a couple more after that before your second ride. You will undoubtedly be standing around in dust, mud, and/or dirt, and let's not even talk about what will happen when you start to groom your horse! Although white, cream, and beige are not the most practical colors for a horse show setting, we must wear them. Here are a few tricks for you to keep clean enough to look presentable every time you go in the ring.

LINT AND DIRT

Get a lint brush or lint roller and use it. You will use this on your coat and on your velvet hat, if that's the kind of hat you wear. You can find these items at dry cleaners, travel stores, and some drug stores and pet stores. An inexpensive alternative is to buy a roll of wide masking tape. Wind a piece around your hand, excluding your thumb, and stick the two ends to each other on the back of your hand. The masking tape will pick up dust and lint just as well as tools made specifically for the job.

Keeping clean: lint roller, lint brush, and Swiffers.

NECKWEAR

Put on your neckwear at the last minute. Don't do all your morning mucking, feeding, and grooming wearing your choker or stock tie (not that you'd want to anyway; they're not all that comfortable to wear even when you have to). Instead, put them on right before you mount. The choker or stock tie is the most noticeable part of what you're wearing under your coat, so even if your shirt's a little dirty, it won't matter that much as long as your choker or stock tie is clean.

BREECHES

If you wear your breeches all day, cover them up with something. Sometimes I see someone wandering around at dressage shows at 6 p.m. in breeches that are still snow-white even though they've been on since early that morning. These are the few and the chosen. The rest of us get dirty. You can keep your breeches clean (beige too!) by wearing a sweats, warm-ups or wind pants, baggy jeans, aprons (cooking or grooming), or long skirts over them. I myself have a floor-length skort, a garment I found at a hunt function boutique that looks like a skirt but actually has two legs like pants. It is dark green and navy plaid with pictures of saddles, bridles, boots, scarlet coats, and hunting whips printed on it. People tend to have extreme reactions to this skort. My (non-horsey) roommate of two years was horrified that I wore it in public, and I have gotten some strange looks in the bagel shops where I'd grab breakfast on my way to the showgrounds. But I have also had many people come up to me at shows who loved the skort—its hunt-themed print is fun and it does a better job of keeping my breeches clean than skirts would, and it's easier to put on and take off than sweats or jeans. I also have a pair of warm-up pants with snaps from hip to heel that are easy to get in and out of.

If your first ride isn't till later in the afternoon and you don't want to have your breeches on all day, you can delay putting them on and thus avoid the problem of how to keep them clean. However, you will have another problem: People's legs tend to swell later in the day, not to mention sweat in the heat. Your breeches may not be as easy to get into in the warm afternoon. This is especially true of full seat breeches, which will likely stick to you instead of sliding on. Solution: Sprinkle baby powder or after-shower powder on your legs and in the legs of the breeches before attempting to put them on. Much easier!

BOOTS

Put your boots on as close to the last minute as possible. Just when this is will vary. If your boots are a smidge too tight, they will go on easier in the morning. Baby powder in the boots will also help. If, like me, you tend to buy your boots a bit generously-sized in the calf to avoid those pre-ride boot pull struggles, you can put your boots on as you're tacking up. However, simply walking the few steps to get from the stall or barn aisle to the mounting block will put at least a little dust on your boots. Once you're in the saddle, have someone run over your boots with a rag, or if you're working by yourself, mount with a rag in your hand, wipe your boots down, and then toss the rag back into your stall or workspace, or tuck it into your breeches or coat if it's small. If you end up having to do much walking around once you've got your boots on, try to walk on grass, avoiding dusty or muddy areas. If you do hit dust or mud, walking through grass (especially slightly dewy grass) will actually clean off your boots for you—the blades of grass act like brush bristles. This works for your horse's feet too. Although I extol the virtues of auto shop rags elsewhere, the best sort of rag to have for dust is a disposable one called a "Swiffer." These magnificent disposable cloths are found in the cleaning section of your grocery store, and they work by using static to pick up dust. You can attach them to a "Swiffer Sweeper" to sweep hard floors, or use them alone for wiping off your boots (and your horse!).

GLOVES

If you're wearing white or light-colored gloves, don't put them on until you're on the horse. Don't try to adjust your bridle and tighten your girth with light gloves on. I guarantee you they will get dirty. Put the gloves in your coat or breeches pocket, or Velcro them to your helmet strap or belt, and put them on once you are settled and your tack is adjusted the way you want it.

KEEPING COOL

Traditional riding attire was designed to keep people warm while foxhunting in the winter in damp, chilly places such as England. With a few minor changes, we still wear essentially the same clothing for competition, but we almost invariably compete in the heat. Although there are winter indoor circuits for the intrepid in the Northeast and the Midwest, for the most part people either stay home in the winter or show where it's warm: Florida, southern California, Mississippi, or Arizona, for example. And in the summer, of course, it can be hot everywhere. So since we're competing in the heat in clothes designed for winter warmth, we need to take steps to keep cool. Overheating, dehydration, heat exhaustion, and heat stroke are dangerous on their own but even more so when you're competing in a physically demanding sport, and the risk of all of these goes up when you involve a horse.

DRINK!

Water is one of your greatest weapons in the battle to keep cool and healthy. Drinking soda doesn't count—it has too much sugar and sodium. Caffeine and alcohol are dehydrating, so if you think you're getting your fluids from your morning coffee and afternoon beer you're not. Alternate your water with an electrolyte sports drink such

as Gatorade, if you like, but avoid using sports drinks exclusively: too much of them may make you nauseous. Drink before you're thirsty—being thirsty means you already are in the early stages of dehydration. Drink until your urine is clear. Drink when you first wake up in the morning, throughout the day, before you ride, and after you ride. This will help keep you cool and safe from the heat. Take a bottle of water with you to the warm-up, and have a few chugs right before you go in the ring. It is surprising how this little bit of extra hydration will clear your mind, cool you down, and make you more ready to attack that test or course. And no, this won't make you have to pee during your ride—you'll be sweating it all out if it's that hot.

KEEP A COOL HEAD

We radiate most of our body heat from our head. So if it's warm, concentrate on your head and neck for keeping cool. That's a difficult feat when youre wearing a black hat with a choker or stock tie around your neck. Get one of those cooling neckbands—these contain little gel beads, and when soaked in water, the beads expand and become cold—they're great for keeping you cooler for hours. Stick your head under a cold hose and cool the back of your neck. Get all your hair soaking wet; it will take a while to dry and will keep you cooler (even under your hat) until it does. Wear a light colored hat when you're not riding. Pale colors deflect heat while dark colors absorb it. And while we're at it, make sure to use plenty of a high SPF sunscreen. Reapply it regularly as indicated on the label; if it's warm you'll sweat it off throughout the day. A sunburn at a show is no fun!

BE A SAVVY SHOPPER

When I'm buying competition attire, I look for clothes that will be relatively cool. My show shirts are made by Romfh, a leader in dressage apparel, and they are made out of Coolmax, a synthetic material that pulls moisture away from the body to keep you cool. Since I show almost exclusively in the warm weather, I bought a coat that is of a very lightweight wool. Manufacturers usually call it "tropical weight wool" or "cool wool" or something of that nature. Cotton is cooler than nylon, so my breeches are cotton.

WAIVED COATS

Don't try to be tough on this one. A hero who has passed out is no good to anyone. According to current USEF rules, if you choose to go coatless when coats are waived, you must wear a short- or long-sleeved shirt (not sleeveless) that is open at the neck with no neckwear (no stock ties or chokers). The shirt should be white or light-colored, and polo shirts are acceptable (but not T-shirts!) Yes, you probably look better in a coat. But if it's hot enough to waive coats, it's probably hot enough that you'll ride much better and much more safely without one. So ditch the coat and take care of yourself.

DRESS MINIMALLY

Although shirt cuffs from long-sleeved shirts look nice under your coat, save them for the cooler early spring and late fall shows. Warm up coatless in a sleeveless shirt and put the coat on at the last minute before you go in the ring. Just make sure to have a short-sleeved shirt on hand in case you luck out and they decide to waive coats—sleeveless shirts are not allowed when coats are waived. I did, however, ride in one show in July in California's Central Valley where the temperature was above 115 degrees; in that case the judge and technical delegate agreed we could wear sleeveless tops. Too bad I didn't have one with me! If you're working alone and don't have someone to hold the coat for you while you're warming up, consider wearing no shirt at all. If you wear a stock tie bib and a coat, no one will know that you're shirtless or that you've only got a sports bra on under that stock tie.

TAKE IT OFF

Once you're done riding, change into cooler clothes as soon as you can. If you can't completely change because you're due back on your horse soon, at least get your coat and hat off for a few minutes. It will make a huge difference. Even if it the air temperature isn't particularly high, you will have heated up considerably from the physical effort of riding and the mental and emotional effort of competing. So cool off.

IF YOU CAN'T TAKE THE HEAT...

Set up a box fan for your horse in his stall, and one for yourself pointing the other direction (or in the tackroom) also. Box fans are available from hardware stores and appliance stores like Sears. They are lightweight, inexpensive, and easy to work. Using baling twine, tie the fan at a comfortable height and plug it in, making sure that the cord (and extension cord, if you use one) are safe from both people and horses. In the tackroom you can have the fan elevated or on the ground. A bucket or bowl of ice set in front of the fan will make the air blown even cooler.

ICE

After you're done warming up and just before you go in the ring, put an ice cube or two down your bra or shirt (the bra works better for women). The ice will melt fairly quickly, but as it melts it will help cool you down. Don't put too much ice in, however; especially at the sitting trot it will clink around and may become distracting.

LADIES ONLY

For many of us women, showing presents a particular challenge at certain times of the month. When we have our period, skintight white or beige pants would not be our apparel of choice—muumuus would feel much better!

CRAMPS

Always make sure you have your preferred painkiller in your trailer, truck, garment bag, or in something that will invariably be with you at shows. For many women who have cramps, over-the-counter solutions such as Tylenol, Advil, or Midol are sufficient. If these do not address your pain sufficiently, see your doctor. There may be some underlying medical condition that needs to be addressed, or you may simply need a painkiller with more oomph. Don't try to be tough on this one, girls; you can't ride if you're doubled over in agony, so get what you need!

BLOATING AND WATER RETENTION

I don't have any snap solution for this one, but just make sure that you have breeches and boots that will still fit you when you are at your puffiest. Although we all prefer to try on clothes when we're feeling svelte, go instead when you are retaining water so that you don't wear yourself out with a pre-ride workout of trying to get dressed!

OTHER PMS SYMPTOMS

Tell people to stay out of your way! No, seriously, if it interferes with your riding or your judgment, seek your doctor's assistance for ways to stabilize your emotions and moods.

MENSTRUAL FLOW

Tampons are your best friend. Use them and you will feel more confident about not ending up with unsightly leaks on your champagne breeches, and you also won't feel like you've got all the cotton in Georgia separating you from your saddle. Although lower absorbency tampons are best for decreasing the risk of toxic shock syndrome, wear the highest ones while you are riding. You can take them out immediately afterward, and they will give you a great deal of peace of mind.

Now let me introduce you to your second best friend: Always Thin Ultra. These pads are super-thin, and instead of cotton which will lump, clump, and bunch uncomfortably and even painfully underneath you as you ride, these pads absorb with a thin layer of material which turns to a gel when wet. The top layer keeps you dry while the interior core absorbs the moisture. The result is that these pads have superior absorbency but feel like you're riding with nothing at all. Even when I'm riding with a tampon, I use an Always Thin Ultra pad as a backup for extra peace of mind.

Wet wipes are great to have as a substitute for hand-washing after you've used the Port-a-Pottie, or for mopping up spills and cleaning you up when your period begins unexpectedly. It is also always a good idea to keep an extra pair of underwear and breeches in the trailer.

If you are on oral contraceptives ("the pill"), you will likely always know when your period is due. It is also possible to manipulate the start of your period by a day or two with your pills if you really don't want to be menstruating during a show.

However, such manipulation may allow you to ovulate during that cycle, which will make your pill ineffective as a contraceptive. Some newer pills allow you to menstruate only four times a year, and Depo-Provera, an injected contraceptive, virtually eliminates your period. Consult your gynecologist or other health care provider before making any changes in contraceptive use.

BARN CLOTHES

At a show, in addition to your competitive apparel, you will need comfortable clothes for working around the barn and simply hanging out. Wear anything that is (a) comfy! (b) okay to get dirty, and (c) easy to get into. Always bring extras; if you're wearing jeans and it rains hard at 7 a.m., you will be miserable by the end of the day if you have nothing to change into! In general, I find jeans, T-shirts, polar fleece, vests, down jackets, silk thermal underwear (if needed), and plenty of rain gear best for cool weather, and loose shorts or cutoffs and sleeveless polos or tank tops best for hot weather.

Always wears closed shoes (no sandals!) around horses for protection in case something is dropped on your foot or you get stepped on. I used to live in paddock boots, but when I got to college I switched to zip-up jodhpur boots because they were quicker to get in and out of. I also found that zippers were less likely to break than boot laces. Now I wear Dansko clogs, which are far and away the most comfortable footwear I've ever encountered! The downside of Dansko clogs is that they provide no protection to the ankle, they are easy to step or twist out of or "fall off" of because they're relatively high, and they tend to accumulate arena footing, shavings or whatever you happen to be walking through. They are also unsafe for riding or longeing since your foot can come out so easily and you can break your ankle with a quick twist (the owner of my barn broke hers this way). Still, Danskos are my shoes of choice around the barn and elsewhere. (I have three pairs and I'm looking to add a few more!) Dansko has also come out with a paddock boot which is high on my "must try" list—if their paddock boots are as superbly comfortable as their clogs, they will have a sure winner.

Barn shoes: Muck Boot Co.'s Tack Classic, Ariat jodhpur boots, Dansko clogs.

The best rainy day footwear I've found is the Muck Boot Co.'s Tack Classic. Unlike most rubber boots I've tried, these boots are very comfortable for walking, and they have the added bonus of keeping my feet warm, so they are what I choose to wear in the winter even when it is not wet out. These boots are also great for mucking stalls, giving baths, or doing coursewalks in muddy or sloppy footing.

THE HORSE

Your Spick-and-Span Horse • Troubleshooting and Spot Cleaning •
Coat and Mane Treatments

YOUR SPICK-AND-SPAN HORSE

GROOMING

When you take your horse to a competition, you will want
him to be as immaculate as possible. However, the most important
parts of your cleaning regimen are your daily grooming and
feeding programs. Proper nutrition and elbow grease produce a
shinier coat than any product you can buy in a bottle at the tack
store! And if you groom well on a daily basis, you will not face
such a daunting task the day before the show.

EVERYDAY GROOMING

For daily grooming, I recommend the following items:
- *Rubber curry comb.* Use in a circular motion to bring up loose
  hair, trapped dirt, caked mud, and dead skin. Knock
  accumulated dirt out of the comb by banging it on the ground,
  the wall (not a clean wall—you will leave marks), or the hard
  back of another brush. Currying is like a massage for horses, and
  many of them love to be curried. Even if I'm really short on
  time, I never skimp on this step before or after riding. I also
  have a small Sof-Touch Grooma that has long, thin, flexible
  rubber teeth which is great for currying sensitive areas such as
  the face and bony areas such as the knees, hocks, and lower legs.
  Rubber grooming mitts also work well for these areas, especially
  the face.
- *Long-bristled dandy brush.* Use this in short strokes with upward
  flicks to remove the hair and dirt produced by the curry comb.
  Stiffer brushes do the job better, but I've found many horses seem
  to find them uncomfortable and prefer softer brushes instead.
- *Short-bristled body brush.* Use long strokes and really put your
  weight into the motion. At the end of each stroke, clean the

body brush by scraping it against a curry comb (rubber or metal). Your work with the body brush will really bring a shine to your horse's coat.

- *Very soft brush*. Use this for brushing sensitive areas such as the legs and face. Some horses like the tiny face brushes that are about the length of your palm; others prefer bigger, soft-bristled brushes on their faces.

- *Soft rag*. I often forego this step on a daily basis, but a rag dampened with water or Bigeloil liniment used in long, weighty strokes will enhance the sheen of your horse's coat and pick up that fine film of dust that the brushes missed. You can wipe the horse's face gently too, including around the eyes, on the lips, and inside the nostrils. Be sure to change to a clean rag every couple of days or so. For the eyes, lips, and nostrils, you can also use big cotton balls or cosmetic squares; since they are disposable, they are more sanitary than a rag is.

- *Hoof pick*. I like the kind that's both a hoof pick and a brush. You can use the brush to loosen caked mud on the outside of the hoof or to tidy up your job after picking the underside. While you're picking out your horse's feet is an ideal time to check on the status of his shoes and feet in general. Does he have any

Grooming equipment (from left): Top row: rubber curry comb, Grooma, Sof-Touch Grooma, dandy brush, blunt-ended scissors. Bottom row: short-bristled body brush, soft face brush, people hair brush, pulling comb, hoof pick with brush.

loose, sprung, or twisted shoes? Are there any clenches risen (nails sticking up a bit instead of flush with the hoof wall)? Are there any cracked or crumbly areas? If a crack is already present, is it getting bigger? Do the feet look long? Horses' hooves grow much faster in the warmer summer months than the cold winter, so keep an eye on them so you can schedule shoeing appropriately. My last horse got shoes every four weeks in the summer, and he really needed them by the fourth week; in the winter, the interval stretched to seven weeks. In the spring and fall, he averaged about six weeks. If you have a concern, discuss your horse's shoeing schedule with your farrier.

- *People hairbrush.* I like the vented kind with sparse plastic bristles for daily mane and forelock brushing. If you brush the mane daily, you won't have to pull it as frequently, because a bit of hair will come out in the hairbrush every day. In terms of tails, I am of the "less brushing is more" school of thought. It takes each tail hair years to reach its full length, and daily brushing (even with a soft body brush) will break hairs and make the tail less full in the long run. I'd rather have a disheveled-looking tail day to day and a full, thick tail at shows than a thin, tangle-free tail every day. On a daily basis, I simply pick or shake out shavings and hay to make the tail a bit tidier. During tick season, which varies geographically, I also make sure to check the tailbone (and the crest of the mane too) for ticks or for open sores with the telltale amber colored crust on the surrounding hair.

IF YOU'RE REALLY IN A HURRY

Although your horse's muscles, skin, and coat benefit from a thorough daily grooming, at times you will be really pressed for time and unable to do the full job. In this case, it's most important to pick out the hooves and take care of the areas under the saddle, girth, and bridle where trapped dirt could cause sores or abrasions. Your horse won't look very snazzy with the mud from this morning's rain caked on his neck as he trots

YOUR SPICK-AND-SPAN HORSE

around the ring, but it won't kill him to go like that every once in a while. Just try not to let it happen too often, and groom him extra well afterwards.

WHEN SHORT ON TIME

Follow this system and you'll have a reasonably presentable horse in moments—you save time by doing everything on one side before switching to the other side, instead of moving back and forth.

Standing on the left side, pick out the left front hoof, then the right front (still from the left side—your horse will soon get used to this). Repeat with the hind hooves, crossing the right hind in front of the left hind.

Take a curry comb in one hand and a short bristled body brush in the other. Starting from the left side upper neck and moving toward the tail, curry the horse, knocking out the dust from your curry comb on the back of the body brush as you go.

Use the body brush on the left side, cleaning it against the teeth of the curry comb after each stroke.

Switch sides and repeat the curry comb and body brush work. As you switch sides, pull obvious shavings or hay out of the tail. Smooth down the mane with the brush as you do the neck.

Stand in front and slightly to the side of the horse and brush off the face and forelock.

METHODS OF RESTRAINT

Horses are easily frightened creatures of flight, and can become especially fidgety if they're uncertain about something we're doing to them, such as clipping, shoeing, sheath cleaning, inoculations, etc. Although they should, and probably will, grow less worried about these activities with time and repetition, some horses are simply too wiggly to stand still, even at ripe old ages. For their safety and ours, we need to have effective methods for keeping them under control.

LEG HOLDING

If the horse is dancing around while you are trying to bandage or clip his legs, the easiest solution is to have someone hold up the opposing leg. Then he must leave his weight on the leg you're working on. Your assistant can hold up the leg by hand or with a sling made of soft rope so the assistant doesn't have to bend over for so long.

STUD CHAIN

Threaded through the halter rings over the nose or over the nose and up the cheek, a stud chain will give you a bit more influence over a horse that's on the edge of out of control, or one that just has his attention elsewhere. A stud chain is probably the best method of restraint when you're not standing still, for example, if you're taking your horse for a walk.

ENCLOSED AREA

Working with your horse in a smaller space (and especially a familiar space, such as the horse's stall) will keep him better under control. For example, giving an injection in the stall with the door closed is very likely going to be much easier than giving one in an open field.

TWITCH

We used to think that twitches worked by causing the horse so much pain on his nose that he forgot about whatever else was happening to him. Now we know that a twitch on the nose releases endorphins, functioning similarly to acupuncture. This second explanation seems more valid: most twitched horses look like they're nearly asleep and don't behave as if they're in pain. If you are working alone, there are nutcracker style twitches, also called "humane" or "one-man" twitches, which can be secured in place with a string and a snap. If you have an assistant, you also have the option of using the sort of twitch that consists of a rod with a loop of rope or chain at the end. To apply the twitch, place the hinge or loop over your left forearm (if you're right-handed). Quickly but gently grasp the horse's muzzle with your left hand and, using your right hand, slide the hinge or loop over your hand and onto the muzzle. Squeeze the nutcracker hinge or twist the loop tightly enough so that the horse's nose cannot slip out. If the horse continues to object to the procedure you're doing, gradually tighten the twitch. In most instances, it will not need to be very tight. Twitches can be used for clipping, braiding, etc., but I advise against using them for anything that involves being near the head, such as clipping the head. Should the horse move his head suddenly, he could inadvertently whack you with the twitch.

Neck Twitch

Some horses are nearly impossible to twitch, and for these I like to use a neck twitch. No special equipment is required. Simply have your helper grab the loose skin on the side of the neck just forward of the shoulder and twist. Most horses will go right to sleep.

Ear Twitch

Ear twitches involve twisting the ear. I don't like to use this method because it tends to make horses very head shy. And when it comes time to clip your horse's ears, you'll be sorry that he won't let you touch them.

Lip Chain

Amelia, my first horse, didn't like being twitched but responded well to a lip chain. I didn't have to even touch it; as long as I had it on her she would stand quietly for anything. Thread a stud chain through the halter rings as you would for an over-the-nose stud chain arrangement, but instead sneak the chain between the upper gum and lip.

TRANQUILIZERS

If none of the methods described above creates a safe enough working environment for the you and your horse, you might resort to tranquilizers. Your vet can advise you on which tranquilizers and what dosages will best suit your needs. Even in less dire circumstances, it is sometimes helpful to use a tranquilizer. For example, a horse that doesn't mind having his sheath touched might nonetheless do well to be tranquilized for a sheath cleaning since this would cause his penis to drop, facilitating the cleaning. But if you're showing, the tranquilizer must be out of his system before you compete. Talk to your vet about how long the tranquilizer will be in the blood before giving your horse anything.

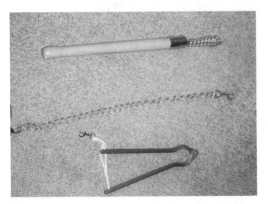

Restraint equipment: chain twitch, chain (stud chain or lip chain), humane (one-man) twitch.

BATHING

Before going to compete, your horse really should have a bath. But sometimes the spring competition season starts before spring has sprung, or there is an early autumn cold snap. Some barns are lucky enough to have heat lamps that the horse can dry under if the weather is chilly, but for the most part the horse should generally not be bathed if the temperature is below fifty degrees or so. Even sixty degrees can seem cold if it's windy. Better to arrive at the showgrounds with a horse that's a bit dirty than one that's caught a chill and is getting sick. I have two suggestions for "bathless bathing."

VACUUMING

Horse vacuums work wonders even on a winter coat with a season's ground-in dirt. Curry your horse very well first, then vacuum him thoroughly. Our barn has an Electro-Groom vacuum that works very well, although at eighty pounds it is a bit heavy to move around much. The same manufacturer has now come out with the Vac-N-Groom, a smaller, more portable vacuum that comes in two sizes. If investing in a horse vacuum is a little pricey for your budget, don't be tempted to grab the wet/dry Shop Vac out of the garage and ask it to do double duty—the excessive noise and strong suction won't serve you well in the barn. Instead, opt for a less powerful (and less expensive) dog or cat grooming vacuum from a pet supply source, or try my next suggestion.

Horse vacuum.

BABY OIL

Fill a five-gallon bucket with warm or hot water, depending on the weather. Squirt an ounce or two of baby oil on the top. Take a large terrycloth towel (already retired from its service as the guest bath towel, please!) and dunk and soak it in the water. The towel will get a little of the bath oil on it, enough to attract dirt from your horse's coat but not enough to leave the coat greasy. Wring out the towel and then rub the horse with the damp towel using a circular motion, finishing by smoothing the hair in the direction of growth. Even though water is involved in this method, your horse won't get soaked to the skin as he would if you were to bathe him, so there is little risk of his getting chilled, particularly if you are working indoors and you cover him up right afterward. He will, however, get surprisingly clean and shiny!

THE TRUE BATH

Using a hose (preferably with a gentle spray setting), hose your horse until he's wet all over. Use water that's comfortable given the ambient temperature—if it's hot out, cool (not cold) water is best; if it's chilly, make the water a bit warmer. In a small bucket, squirt the amount of shampoo as directed on the bottle and fill with water (put the shampoo in first so that the agitation of the water from the hose creates suds). I prefer concentrated shampoos; my favorites are Orvus, Absorbine Superpoo, Rio Vista and Cowboy Magic, in no particular order. All four produce a nice lather, do a good job of removing dirt, and rinse well, leaving the coat soft

Bathing equipment (from left): Top row: Cowboy Magic detangler, shampoo, Pledge, Selsun Blue, baby oil. Bottom row: grooming mitt, Grooma Loopa, sponge.

and shiny. Shampoos that don't rinse out well (or these if you don't use enough water!) will make the coat look dull when dry. Using a sponge, grooming mitt, Grooma Loopa shampoo mitt, car washing mitt, or a combination, soap the horse all over using a circular motion, rubbing to get to the dirt at the skin. I usually use a bit of shampoo drizzled full strength on the top part of the tail, then dunk the skirt in the bucket and lather well. I may also use the shampoo full strength on the mane and legs, depending on how dirty they are. Rinse the horse well until you can scrape him with a sweat scraper and not produce any bubbles.

My rule of thumb for washing horses' faces is that you shouldn't get any more soap on them than you're sure you can get off. Although some horses tolerate or even enjoy it, most object to having their faces hosed. If you don't know where your horse stands on this, turn the water down so the spray is more gentle and begin by spraying your horse's upper neck. Casually creep toward his cheek. If he doesn't object, continue on the side of his head toward his nose and mouth, and then try the forehead from one side or the other. If he gets worried, back off for a moment and then try again, patting him and speaking to him softly. Some horses seem to object to the hose less if you dribble the water between the ears and down the center of the face. Let your horse drink out of the hose when he is hot after a ride so that he starts to think of water on his face as a good, not a scary, thing. If you work at it gradually over a series of baths, he will probably become more and more comfortable with the process.

Another option is to try sponging. My horse Donovan hated having his face sprayed, but he didn't mind if I held a dripping-wet sponge on his forehead and squeezed water all over his face. Go figure. Sponge bathing the face is just as effective as hosing, and your horse may like it better. Experiment and find what works best for him. Remember, the point is to get him clean, not to get him clean in a specific way.

If your horse is a real loon about water on his face no matter what you try, you may have to use one of the methods of restraint described earlier to get the job done. Or you may be able to get that part of him adequately clean with your Soft-Touch Grooma, face brush, and damp cloth.

Once you've rinsed and sweat-scraped your horse, it's time to put conditioner on his tail. Before a show is the only time I make an exception to the no-tail-brushing rule. As great as they may look on people, the judge does not want to see dreadlocks in your horse's tail as he's going down the long side! I used to use rinse-out moisturizing or detangling conditioners for human hair (Salon Selectives and Pantene work well) on my horses' tails, but now I'm absolutely hooked on Cowboy Magic's detangler. It really does seem like magic—the no-rinse product leaves your horse's tail soft and shiny, and it remains tangle-free and easy to brush for the entire show weekend. Work a small amount of the gel-like substance through your horse's tail as per the instructions on the bottle (if you use too much, the tail will be greasy). Now is the time to hand-pick out any knots you may see, but leave the brushing until the tail is dry. Wet hair stretches and breaks more easily than dry hair (this goes for people hair too!)

WHEN TO BATHE

If your horse isn't the type that likes to roll in the mud or he doesn't have the option to do so, bathe him about two days before he'll be competing (usually the day before you leave). This will give the natural oils in his skin a chance to replenish themselves, and the good groomings you'll give him in the interim will distribute them, making him shinier than if he were fresh-bathed. With mud muffins, if the weather's warm enough I wash the horse the day I leave and let him dry while I load up the trailer (be sure you never transport a wet horse if it's even slightly cool—he may get chilled). Once at the show he stays clean because I pick his stall constantly and there's no turnout for him to get muddy in. In cooler weather, I wash him the day before we leave and pray that there will be adequate bathing facilities on the showgrounds (although you should never bank on it unless you have been to the facility before). If there aren't, you can always use the baby oil method described above. If this competition is your first of the spring season and your horse hasn't been bathed since his last autumn show, you may want to do a two-part bath, the first about a week before you leave, and once more the day before you leave. You will be surprised how much dirt you can get off a horse that hasn't had a bath in several months, even if he's been groomed religiously!

TROUBLESHOOTING AND SPOT CLEANING

HOOVES

You can give your horse's hooves a rudimentary cleaning by scrubbing them with a sponge dunked in your sudsy shampoo bucket. However, to get them really clean, use a dishwashing brush squirted with Palmolive or Dawn dish soap and scrub away. Clean hooves have an astonishing way of making the whole horse look cleaner and sharper. When I was a working student in Germany, we prepared horses for an in-hand mare show at the Hanoverian Verband simply by scrubbing their hooves and washing their tails. Their manes got braided and we gave them a good grooming, but we only washed feet and tails. And they looked surprisingly nice!

Before you go into the show ring, you will want to put a little something on your horse's hooves to make them look extra spiffy. What you put on depends on what surface you'll warm up and show on. If both the warm-up and show ring are grass, you can use hoof oil (applied after leaving your stall please—otherwise you'll take half your shavings or straw with you!). Fiebing's hoof dressing or Rainmaker are good. You can do the same if you warm up on grass and show in sand or other loose footing. If you warm up on sand, stonedust, or dirt, however, the arena footing will stick to conventional hoof dressing and make the hooves look unkempt. If you have someone helping you, you can warm up with nothing on the hooves and have your helper add hoof oil once you've finished your warm-up and are waiting to go into the competition ring.

Another option is to use hoof polish, a good choice if the footing is very fine and dusty. Absorbine Supershine is a good one, and it is easily removable with liniment. (Please remember to remove the hoof polish—it is very hard on the hooves.) Products like Tuff Stuff, a hoof toughener and conditioner, also dry quickly and leave the hooves looking shiny. My farrier uses high gloss, clear acrylic spray from the hardware store instead and swears it works just as well (it is also much more economical). When compared with hoof polish, Tuff Stuff and acrylic spray are the better options: they can enhance the hooves' health, you don't have to take them off, and they give as nice a shine as hoof polish does.

My usual choice for show-ring ready hooves is a little simpler. I put a little corn oil or baby oil on a soft rag and rub it on the hooves. A few minutes later, I buff it to a shine with a clean dry rag. This treatment repels dirt and arena footing and leaves the hooves with a natural-looking shine. But the buffing step is important—if you forget to do it, the oil will be a magnet for dirt and dust instead of a repellent.

Hoof shining: baby oil, hoof oil, rag for buffing and wiping.

WHITE MARKINGS

Romi, my second horse, was a bay with four white stockings all the way up to his knees and hocks, plus a big white blaze. Striking, yes, but monstrous to keep clean! As a result of my years with Romi, I learned a few surefire ways to keep those white markings white.

QUIC SILVER, QUIC SILVER, QUIC SILVER!

This is a godsend for anyone whose horse has any white, anywhere. I have tried other whitening shampoos and none of them comes even close. Quic Silver shampoo goes on purple and rinses away to leave your horse's white or gray hair with a lovely silver shimmer. Use it multiple times or leave it on for several minutes before rinsing to get even better results. I always wore gloves (disposable latex—you can buy them by the box at the

Caring for white markings: Quic Silver, baby powder, Betadine (to be combined with Orvus), cornstarch.

drugstore) while using Quic Silver; it dried my hands out and tinted them purple if I used it barehanded.

BLUING

Remember little blue-haired old ladies? Use their secret: liquid bluing! Available at drug stores and some tack stores, liquid bluing (Mrs. Stewart's is a brand I recommend) is excellent at removing manure and urine stains and whitening yellowed gray tails.

ORVUS AND BETADINE SURGICAL SCRUB

The owner of my barn mixes Orvus shampoo with Betadine to get her horses' white markings white. The advantage of this option over Quic Silver or bluing is that it won't dry out the horse's skin as much, and if he has got any sort of mild bacterial or fungal skin problems cooking, the Betadine's antiseptic and antimicrobial properties will help counteract those as well.

CORNSTARCH

Another method for getting your whites sparkling white is rubbing cornstarch into the hair while it's still wet. Allow the hair to dry, then brush out the remaining cornstarch. For best results, I use cornstarch in combination with either Quiksilver or bluing. The combination produces better results than either method would alone.

CLIPPING

Especially if your horse has set and reset stains in long winter hair all season, your best bet for getting him white may be clipping to uncover the cleaner hair closer to the skin. This option is most useful on legs. Use a #10 blade (anything finer will turn your horse's white to pink) and clip several days to a week before your show. Doing your clipping early will give the hair the opportunity to outgrow the fresh shorn look, and you can maintain the newly white legs with the methods mentioned above if needed.

COAT PROBLEMS

DANDRUFF

Romi was not the easiest horse to prepare for a Pony Club formal inspection (and this was not for lack of practice—he went to my C2, C3 and B ratings, two National Championships, and a variety of regional rallies in addition to doing dressage shows and events). Not only did he have lots of chrome, he also had a perpetually dandruffy tail. It never seemed to itch or bother him in any way, but I was not going to lose my team horse management points or fail a rating because of dandruff in my horse's tail, of all things!

Dandruff Shampoos

I tried lots of dandruff shampoos with Romi over the years (both people and horse shampoos), but the best by far is Selsun Blue. Why? I have no idea. But it works. Use full strength and massage into the horse's tail right at the skin of the tailbone and in other dandruff-prone areas (the elbows and mane, for example). Allow the suds to sit several minutes, then rinse and repeat.

Listerine

I was thumbing through a book of ads from the early 1900s and ran across one for Listerine. "Use Listerine for dandruff!" it proclaimed. I was surprised—I had been using Listerine on my horses' dandruff for years but I never knew that it was ever an "official" use of the product. Put Listerine (the plain kind) in a spray bottle and spray directly on affected areas, parting the hair to rub it in with your fingertips. Allow the Listerine to sit for up to an hour, then rinse, shampoo, and condition as usual. The dandruff seems to dissolve. I particularly like to use the Listerine treatment in conjunction with Selsun Blue for best results.

Shedding

If your horse is transitioning between winter and summer coats and has an unsightly combination of both, douse him completely in baby oil and let it sit overnight. The next morning, bathe him with warm water. The old loose hair will come right out, leaving him looking sleek and seasonable.

Bald Spots

If your horse had a scrape or some other incident that caused him to lose a patch of hair, try applying Rogaine. I have never had the need to use it on my horses (they have all regrown lost hair very quickly), but my barn manager swears by it. You can buy Rogaine at drug stores or places like Costco. The owner of my barn has had good luck with Horseman's Dream veterinary cream as well.

LEG FUNGUS

I have tried many remedies for that stubborn, crusty, bumpy fungus (the kind where the hair looks raised and will come out in big chunks) that some horses get on their hind legs (particularly in the summer), but I have only found one that was effective. The second summer I had him, Donovan got the worst case I had ever seen. I treated it for one week with this concoction and it never returned. Combine one-half tub Furazone (the yellow ointment used for cuts and for leg sweating) with an equal part Desitin (the diaper rash ointment you can find at your drugstore) and 2 cc of liquid DMSO (you can buy this from a vet supply catalog). So as not to absorb the harsh DMSO through your own skin, apply with latex gloves once a day for several days to a week, depending on the severity of the fungus.

Ingredients for leg fungus remedy: liquid DMSO, Furazone, Desitin.

SHEATH AND UDDERS

If you had a horse in Pony Club that was prone to kick, you considered yourself lucky at formal inspection time. The horse management judge would often eye the threatening hind leg and decide that self-preservation was more important than seeing just how good a job you did of cleaning the horse's sheath or udders. Those of us with agreeable horses had no choice but to learn to clean sheaths and udders well. Judges would put their hand inside the sheath and scrape with their fingernails—and they had better not find any dirt or accumulated grime or you would be out some points! (Even for those Pony Clubbers with kickers, you could never be sure when you'd get a clever or just plain crazy horse management judge who would check anyway, so it was always best to have at least a moderately clean sheath or udder area no matter what.)

PICKING

If you pull the major chunks of accumulated dead skin, dirt, and secretions off your horse's sheath or udders on a weekly basis or so, the area should stay clean enough that there won't be problems with swelling and irritation caused by lack of cleanliness. Still, you should wash the sheath or udders periodically anyway.

WASHING

It is not necessary to buy pricey, specially formulated sheath cleaners, but if you do, Excalibur is a good one. Instead, you can use a mild soap like Ivory or a small bar of glycerine soap and a bucket of warm water, along with practical cotton or a small tack cleaning sponge. Wear latex gloves to keep your fingernails from scratching the horse's sensitive skin, and to keep your hands from picking up the strong odor. It is easiest to clean the sheath when your horse's penis is completely dropped down. Some horses will drop down when they're relaxed, as in when they're snoozing or getting groomed, but they may not remain dropped down once you start working on cleaning the area. Tranquilization is the surest way of getting the horse to drop down and stay that way for the duration of the cleaning. Additionally, many horses are fussy about having their sheath or udders handled, so tranquilization will make the process safer for you. Your vet can give your horse an injection, or you can give him an oral tranquilizer previously obtained from your vet. (If you plan to give injections yourself, be aware that in the event of a complication, having received an injection from someone other than a vet will probably void your horse's insurance policy. Also, make sure that you have been properly trained on how to give an injection by your vet or another knowledgeable person, and that you dispose of the used needles and syringes appropriately.) It is possible to do a sheath cleaning without the horse dropping down; if you clean it this way you must be extra careful that you have rinsed all the soap away to prevent irritation inside the sheath.

Once your horse is prepared and you have your materials assembled, sponge or hose the area with warm water. Using your cotton, sponge, or a wet bar of glycerine soap, gently rub to loosen and soften crusty buildup between the udders, in the sheath, and on the penis. Especially important to remove is the "pea" or "bean," the buildup at the head of the penis that can block the urethra and cause problems with urination. Be sure to rinse well. Do not do a full-scale sheath or udder cleaning too frequently, since constant cleansing can actually cause an increase in the secretion of oils that contribute to buildup. If you do maintenance work on a regular basis, you should not need to wash the sheath or udders more frequently than once every couple of months.

CHESTNUTS

Chestnuts are the crusty growths horses develop inside the hocks and above the knees. You can usually peel or pick them off until they are nearly flush with the horse's hair, and that's all that's necessary to make them presentable. However, for an extra touch you can rub baby oil into them to darken them. This looks especially nice on darker horses or chestnut-colored ones.

SHOW RING SHINE

When I competed in rallies as a Pony Clubber, we were always warned by our club leaders beforehand not to arrive at the rally with coat polishes on our horses. These have a drying effect on the hair and also make it more slippery, which compromises safety if used in the saddle area. We also heard (although I do not know if it can be substantiated or not) that coat polishes do not allow the coat to breathe and they impair the horse's ability to sweat, robbing him of his natural cooling mechanism. Whether or not we believed that all coat polishes were evil, we quickly learned not to use them at Pony Club competitions. They leave such a distinctive slippery plastic feel to the coat that horse management judges could tell immediately whether we had used them, which of course resulted in penalty points. So here's my substitute: Pledge furniture polish.

Pledge? Yes, Pledge. One might think it strange that a furniture polish would be safe and effective as a substitute coat polish, but Pledge's main action (including on furniture) is as a dust repellent, so this works for keeping horses clean, too. You can use either the pump spray or aerosol variety. Spritz it on the tail to help keep it clean and tangle free without the drying effects of conventional coat polishes. Use it on your horse's body to keep him shiny and repel dust without making him slick (although I would still refrain from applying it under the saddle). Spray some on a soft clean rag and wipe it on his face, avoiding the area above the eyes so that it doesn't get in the eyes and irritate them when he sweats. I used Pledge at all the rallies and ratings I went to, and not one examiner or horse management judge noticed anything out of the ordinary, except maybe that I had a spotlessly clean horse!

COAT AND MANE TREATMENTS

TRIMMING

How you trim your horse in preparation for a show depends on the type of competition you're going to. Even (or especially) if you're going to a smaller local show or schooling show, plan to turn your horse out appropriately. Not only does it reflect well on you as a horseman and a serious competitor respectful of the sport, it keeps your horse looking tidy and keeps your clipping and pulling skills in practice for the important competitions. You can trim with small- to medium-sized clippers, or you can also use blunt-ended scissors for many areas such as fetlocks and tailbones.

HUNTERS

Trimming required for hunters is more detailed than for any other discipline.
- Clip fetlocks and around coronet bands (you can also "boot up" the horse if you like)
- Pull mane to 4-5 inches and a thickness appropriate for braiding
- Leave tail natural (no pulling or banging) and braid
- Clip scraggly hairs under jaw, muzzle whiskers, eye whiskers
- Clip narrow bridle path (slightly wider than width of crownpiece of bridle)
- Clip ears out

DRESSAGE HORSES

- Clip fetlocks and around coronet bands
- Pull mane as for hunters, or with traditionally long-maned breeds (e.g., Arabians, Andalusians) leave mane long for French braiding
- Pull or clip the sides of the tailbone at the top, continuing about one third of the way down the tailbone (although some dressage horses now go with unpulled but banged tails)
- Bang the tail so that when it is slightly raised during movement, it falls at or just above the fetlocks
- Clip narrow bridle path to accommodate bridle (for Arabians left with their manes long it may continue further down the neck, about one-quarter of the way down, or six to eight inches)
- Clip under jaw; it is appropriate to leave muzzle and eye whiskers long after the style in Europe
- Tidy up the edges of the ears (you do not need to clip them out)

EVENT HORSES

Event horses are trimmed as dressage horses except that tails are often banged shorter (just below the hock), they are pulled farther down the tailbone, and muzzle whiskers are usually clipped. Putting up a long mane in a French braid is not seen as frequently in eventing as in dressage; unless you need to leave the mane long because you also show in breed classes, it is advisable to pull the mane if eventing is your primary sport.

JUMPERS

Jumpers may be turned out in the style of hunters, or in the European style (including loose forelocks) reflected in dressage turnout. Often jumper manes are left unbraided, with fairly thick manes that are one to two inches longer than conventional pulled manes. Although this casual style is becoming more commonplace even in the big Grands Prix, braiding is never incorrect.

An untrimmed horse.

The same horse trimmed for jumpers, dressage, or eventing. Note pulled mane, tidied ears, clipped muzzle and jaw line, clipped fetlocks, pulled and banged tail.

MANE PULLING

Unless you have an Arabian, Lusitano, Andalusian, or other traditionally long-maned horse, you must have a pulled mane for any

of the disciplines discussed in this book, although the desired length and thickness may vary. A pulled mane is shorter and thinner than a mane left on its own, and it is thicker at the roots than at the ends. You can accomplish this several ways.

TRADITIONAL

Back-combing the mane toward the roots for pulling.

Most horses don't object to having their mane hair actually pulled out, although thinner-skinned horses such as Thoroughbreds can be sensitive about it. Grab a hunk of mane and comb it from roots to end with a small metal pulling comb. Then, holding on to the longest part, comb the rest up and back toward the roots (like teasing hair). Now you will have a much smaller amount of

Winding the mane around the comb to pull.

hair between your fingers. Wind this once around the comb near the roots for leverage, and yank. Comb the hair back into place. With a more sensitive horse, be careful to only pull out a few hairs with each yank and he will probably object less. Repeat up and down the length of the neck until the mane is of the desired length and thickness, remembering that you can always pull out a little more but you can't glue it back on if you've taken too much away.

GROOMA MANEMASTER

This tool was invented for horses that don't like having their manes pulled. You comb down and then back as you would with a pulling comb, but then you squeeze the Manemaster and it cuts the selected hair near its roots. Although this isn't a bad solution if you don't plan to braid, the cut hair will stick up and get spiky as it grows out and ruin the line of your braids. Steel used to be horrible about having his mane pulled. This usually mild-mannered horse would throw people against walls and generally have a fit during the procedure. To get him more reasonable about the whole enterprise, I would try to pull his mane every day, but just one or two hairs so he would get used to the idea. During that time I used other methods (a Manemaster or scissors) for actually shortening and thinning his mane, and eventually he got laid back enough about having his mane pulled that I could do it the traditional way, although I was careful to take only a few hairs in each yank.

"Pulling" with a Grooma Manemaster.

SCISSORS

Although you can use scissors for thinning (comb down and then up with a pulling comb, and cut), they will present the same problems of spikiness as the Manemaster. So I prefer to use them only for shortening. Romi had an extraordinarily thin mane, and if

I pulled it to shorten it at all he'd have no mane left and I'd have nothing to braid. Instead, I used scissors to shorten it. To get a mane that looks and feels as good as a pulled one, hold the scissors parallel to the hairs of the mane, snipping off little bits of the hair gradually so that the mane looks and feels

Trimming the mane with scissors held vertically.

as if it were pulled (i.e. thinner at the ends of the hair than at the roots). If you hold the scissors perpendicular to the mane, you will end up with a mane that's impossible to braid and a horse that looks like he's had a close encounter with a lawn mower. You can also use thinning shears (purchased from a hair styling shop), but, although quicker, these will not leave the mane looking as natural.

BRAIDING

Relax when you are first learning to braid—it's really not that hard! If you can braid people hair you can definitely braid horse hair; it's much coarser and less slippery and therefore easier to work with. If you haven't learned to braid people hair, I suggest that you practice using three lead ropes. It's easier to learn the mechanics of basic braiding when you don't have to worry about keeping the three sections of hair separate. Clip the three lead ropes to a hook or something on the wall and fan them out so that you have one on the left, one in the middle, and one on the right. Bring the right hand rope over the center rope. Now that rope is your new center rope. Now bring the left rope over the center rope. Then the right one, then the left, and so on. Once you've got that down, concentrate on keeping the existing braid tight and even as you continue to work. And now you know how to braid!

BRAID MAINTENANCE

Hunter braids are among the easiest to maintain and, despite the name, are appropriate for all disciplines discussed in this book: hunter, jumper, dressage, and eventing. They look good on virtually any horse, and they are very secure. You can leave them in for the whole weekend if your horse doesn't try to rub them out on the frame of the door (edges work best for braid elimination). To help prevent rubbing, make sure the mane is very clean and dandruff-free (and well rinsed) so that the horse is itch-free before you begin braiding. Some horses simply dislike the feeling of braids in their manes and will rub them even if their manes don't itch. In these cases, you can put a web stall guard above the lower half of the Dutch doors that are common at horse shows, or, if there is one, you can close the top half of the Dutch door. I prefer the stall guard method because it allows the horses to see out and doesn't restrict ventilation. Horses often get nervous if they are completely shut in. If you have a bona fide mane rubber, however, he will probably find something to rub on no matter what—his water buckets, the wall, his hind foot. For this horse, you will have to plan to redo the braids every morning and try to keep an eye on him in between rides.

There are nylon, Lycra, and polyester hoods, such as the Sleazy, Jammies, or RobinHoods that protect braids by covering your horse's head, neck, and shoulders, but I don't often use them. I usually compete in warm enough weather that I don't want to add a layer on my horse, and all my horses have generally done a good job taking care of their braids anyhow. Hoods are be excellent at keeping shavings, hay, straw, or debris out of the braids, but they tend to give the braids a smashed, flat look. Plus, a dedicated mane rubber can still make his braids scruffy and unkempt-looking even with a hood on. Even if your horse doesn't rub, he will probably end up with some hay or bedding in his braids if they're left in overnight. Use a small face brush to gently brush away fine particles on top of, around, and underneath the braid.

For those who want to avoid braiding and braid maintenance entirely, you can roach your horse's mane: if your horse has a nice neck and you don't like to grab mane during bobbles or over jumps, it is acceptable to completely clip it off for dressage, eventing, or jumpers (not hunters!) The big downside of roaching a mane is that it will come back in thick, bristly, and unruly if you ever decide to grow it out again, making for some difficult braiding. Roached manes are probably most commonly seen in dressage, though even there they are rare. The forelock is left loose, or it can be put up in a braid. But your horse had better have a great neck if you want to go the roaching route!

BRAIDING EQUIPMENT

You don't need to get one of those special braiding kits from the tack store. If you assemble your own you will, for a better price, have exactly the tools you need and none of the superfluous ones.

Spray bottle or small tack sponge and bucket—Many horses get nervous about spray bottles near their ears; most don't object to the sponge.

Water or Quic Braid

I usually braid with plain water although Quic Braid (from the folks who brought us Quic Silver, bless their souls!) works very well. If you plan to keep your braids in for several days or you're working with a slippery mane that's hard to hold onto, give Quic Braid a try. Some people use hair gel, but I find it awkward to work with. It makes the hair sticky and slick and dries a bit crusty (and it can be itchy). I haven't had any sticky, slick, crusty, or itchy problems with Quic Braid. Or with water, for that matter.

Plastic Comb

You can find inexpensive, plain, fine-toothed combs in the drugstore or supermarket.

Hair Clips

Use the long metal kind that hair stylists use when they're cutting your hair and want to keep sections out of the way. You can find these at beauty supply stores or in the haircare section of most drugstores and some supermarkets.

Yarn (for hunter braids)

Go to a craft store and buy yarn that matches your horse's mane. There are a few brands that make a great chestnut-colored yarn, but dark brown usually blends in too if you can't find chestnut. Black is always easy to find for bays and blacks. For grays, use black or some shade of gray, depending on how dark your horse's mane is. White usually stands out too much unless the mane is truly snow-white.

Rubber Bands (for European braids)

This is one item that I refuse to skimp on. I buy Super Bands (available from Stateline Tack's catalog and from some tack stores). They are more expensive than any other braiding rubber bands I've seen, but they are also incredibly strong and durable, and they don't stretch more than they need to. Buy them to match your horse's mane or in white.

Waxed Braiding Thread (for sewn-in braids)

This is usually available in brown or black. I prefer waxed thread to unwaxed because it's easier to use and seems to be stronger. You can buy this thread from Bit of Britain or from local tack shops that cater to event riders.

Pull Throughs (for hunter and sewn-in braids)

At your craft store, buy a pull through used for making latch hook rugs. They are far easier to use than the plastic sticks with loops at the end. Some tack stores also carry good pull throughs.

Seam Ripper

Again, you can purchase this from your craft or sewing store. You will use this on all varieties of braids, including rubber banded ones.

Small Scissors

Choose small, blunt-ended ones from a drugstore or craft store. High quality children's scissors (e.g., Fiskars) do the job well.

Head Lamp or Glasses

At an outdoor/camping store you can find a hands-free light that you strap to your head. I also have glasses with flashlights on either side, which I bought at a hardware store. Although not absolute necessities all the time, it is invaluable to have these available if you should ever find yourself braiding in the dark or simply in poor lighting.

Step Stool

You can get this at a hardware store. Don't go big and fancy; a little, sturdy one will be sufficient to get you high up enough to braid most horses' manes. The top of my stool opens to reveal a compartment where I store all the rest of my braiding paraphernalia. It also doubles as a mounting block. Nifty, huh?

Braiding equipment (from left): Top row: Super Bands, flashlight glasses, yarn. Bottom row: scissors, seam ripper, comb, white tape, hair clip, pull through.

HUNTER BRAIDS

There are several different methods for doing hunter braids, but this one is simple and effective. If you are only going to learn to do one type of braiding, it should be this kind because you can take a hunter braid virtually anywhere: any discipline, any horse. I have used these braids at hunter/jumper shows, at events, and at dressage shows as well.

Prepare yarn by winding it from the palm of your hand around your elbow and around to your palm, then your elbow again, continuing until you have gone around about thirty times. Cut through all the yarn at your palm. You will now have about thirty pieces of yarn twice the length of your forearm. Stick the pieces of yarn through the ring on your horse's halter so they're handy.

Starting at the poll, dampen several inches of mane with sponge or spray. Comb through dampened area, and neatly part the first section of mane, usually about an inch in width. Clip back the adjacent mane with a hair clip. How wide the section will be depends on how thin the mane is and what sport you're doing. Hunters usually go in about thirty to forty small braids. Dressage and event horses in hunter braids usually go in about twenty to thirty larger braids. Play around over several different shows and find out what looks best on your horse. Generally, horses with too-short necks should have more braids to elongate the neck, and long-necked horses should have fewer braids to make them look more balanced. However wide you decide to make each section of mane, it is important that the braids be as evenly spaced and sized as possible.

Divide the section of mane into three equal sections. Fold one piece of yarn in half. Place the yarn under the three sections of mane so that the halfway point is directly under the center section. The right-hand half of the yarn should be braided in as part of the section that begins as the right-hand section, and the left-hand half of the yarn is now part of the left-hand section. Braid the hair down as far as possible, pulling downward as you go and keeping the tension tight and even. At the end, pinch the tip of the braid in your left hand and take the two ends of yarn to the right and behind the braid, creating a loop to the right of the braid. Pull the ends of yarn across the front of the braid and through the loop and tighten. You have now tied a slipknot around the end of the braid. Do another slipknot. Continue braiding sections of mane until you have finished.

Insert your pull through with the hook open into the top of the braid at the crest of the neck. Capture the end of the yarn in the hook and close it. Pull the pull through back up through the braid (but take care not to pull too far—it's easy to pull the end of the braid through the top). Now the two ends of yarn are on the top side of the braid. Separate the ends, one around the underside of braid to the right, one to the left, and cross them underneath. Bring the ends around to the front

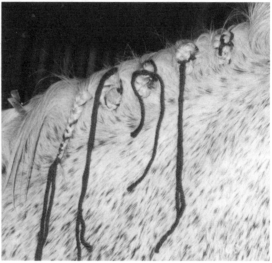

Hunter braids. 1) Section of mane divided into three portions. 2) Yarn braided into mane and tied at the end. 3) Yarn pulled through the top of the braid. 4) Yarn ends separated and crossed around the back to tie in the front. 5) Braid tied with a surgeon's knot. 6) Completed braid with yarn ends trimmed off.

side again and tie across the front of the braid, one-third of the way from the top. Do not tie the yarn perfectly horizontal; instead let it go parallel to one of the sections of the braid. This will keep the finished braid from twisting. Use a surgeon's knot in tying off the yarn. This is simply a square knot with an extra twist. Take the right-hand end of yarn and cross it over the left piece of yarn and pull it through (exactly like the first step in tying shoelaces). Then repeat this step: right over left and pull through again. This is what makes it

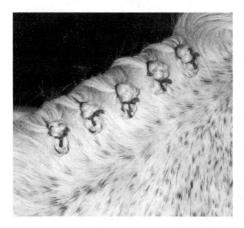

A completed row of hunter braids.

a surgeon's knot. Now cross the left end over the right end and pull through. The knot will often look loose but will rarely come undone, unlike the square knot which looks tighter but is more likely to untie itself. Snip off the ends of the yarn (but not too close to the knot!).

You can do the forelock in the same manner as the mane, except that you begin with a French braid and add the yarn once the French braid is done and you are finishing the ends in a regular braid. For a French braid, you begin with three sections of forelock, but add a little more forelock from the side as you braid down. When you're crossing the right section over the center, you add in a little more hair from the right; when you're crossing the left section over the center, you add from the left. The braid will look better if you add hair in very small sections. Once you've incorporated all the hair into the braid, add in the yarn. Finish and tie up as usual. Alternatively, you can pull the entire length of the braid up through the French braided part and tie it off up there.

EUROPEAN BRAIDS

I learned to do these braids as a working student in Germany. In Europe you see rubber banded braids on the fanciest Grand Prix horses at the biggest shows. At first I was horrified at the idea of using rubber bands for braiding (I had always been taught that this was a major fashion faux pas!), but the finished braids set off the neck nicely. Instead of lying flat like hunter braids, they stand out a bit from the neck. Although many people find European braids faster and easier to put in, I find I can do hunter braids more quickly, probably because I've had more practice with them.

Using a fairly large section of damp mane (usually about one and a half inches—you will finish with fewer and larger braids than typical hunter braids), braid till the end and tie off with a rubber band. On the last twist of the rubber band, turn the unbraided end up with the rubber band so that it lies along the braid instead of sticking out below. I find it helpful to keep a rubber band on my left pinkie so I don't have to go rummaging while trying to keep the braid from unraveling. But I never put on more than one or two at a time or my pinkie starts to turn purple!

Mentally divide the braid into thirds from top to bottom. Fold the bottom third of the braid under the middle third. Now fold the combined bottom and middle third under the top third. You will now have a folded up braid a third of the length of the original braid. It should stick out almost perpendicular to the neck. Using a second rubber band, join all three thicknesses of the braid together, keeping the band as close to the crest as possible. Wrap the band around three or more times, depending on the thickness of the braid, making sure that there are no gaps of mane showing between each

European banded braids. 1) Section of mane braided and finished with a rubber band. 2) Braid folded into thirds. 3) Folded braid held in place with another rubber band.

turn of the rubber band. Particularly if you are using white bands, it is important for the band to be in the same location on each braid so that the appearance of the topline is balanced and even.

With this style of braids it is appropriate either for the forelock to be French braided and put up with rubber bands like the mane or for it to be left loose. A loose forelock is flattering on a horse with a large or coarse head, but only if the forelock is reasonably full. Very thin forelocks look better braided.

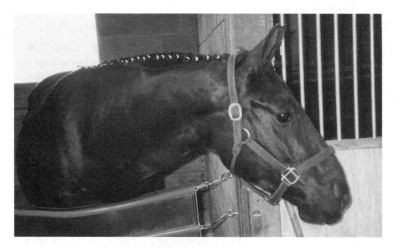

European banded braids with white tape.

RUNNING FRENCH BRAID

Cindy, a horse I leased before I bought my first horse, was a Morgan/Arabian cross (we think). At any rate, the owner didn't want her mane pulled, so I used a French braid when I competed at local shows. Although Susan Harris (my grooming guru who wrote the classic *Grooming to Win* plus the more recent USPC manuals) recommends keeping the braid tight and close to the crest, I find that the horse has more freedom in the neck (important in dressage in the free walk or extended walk, and also in the "stretchy-chewy" circle) if you start at the poll with the braid tight at the crest and gradually move away from the crest as you braid down. Try it both ways and find what works best for you and your horse.

Begin by separating three sections of mane at the poll, about three-quarters of an inch each. Cross the right over center, left over center, right over center like we've been doing with the other braids. Then when you cross the left section over the center the next time, add another three-quarter inch section of mane. Continue adding three-quarter inch sections to the left section each time until all the mane is incorporated in the braid. Finish the braid off with a rubber band, and turn the ends of the mane up in the rubber band (or in a second rubber band) so that the end of the braid is neat. You can also pull the braid up as in a hunter braid, but I prefer the rubber band method. Leave the forelock loose, or, if you like, put it up as you would for hunter or European braids.

SEWN-IN BRAIDS (BUTTON BRAIDS)

I have only recently begun doing sewn-in braids at events. Although the sewing-in process is a bit time consuming, they will stay in better than even hunter braids. They look particularly nice on Thoroughbred-type event horses. Their only drawback is that they take forever and a day to undo—you must be very handy (and patient!) with a seam ripper to get these suckers out!

You will need thread made specifically for braiding; you can find it at event-oriented tack stores such as Bit of Britain, and the waxed kind is easiest to work with. You will also need a large, dull-pointed tapestry needle which you can get from craft stores. In order to have enough thread to work with comfortably, I use lengths twice as long as I would for hunter braids (that is, from my hand around my elbow back to my hand and then repeat), although one and a half times the length would probably be sufficient.

Braid the thread into the mane and tie off the ends as you would for hunter braids. You can use a wider chunk of mane for each braid with sewn-in braids; approximately one and a half to two inches, depending on the length and thickness of the mane and neck. Once you've braided and tied off all the braids, thread the needle with the thread from the first braid. Stitch once up through the base of the braid at the neck (the same location where you would pull the yarn up in hunter braids). Then make several stitches down the length of the braid and back up again, ending with the threaded needle at the center of the top side of the base of the braid. Roll the braid up under itself, cinnamon roll style, and

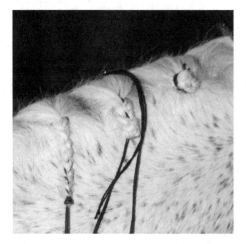

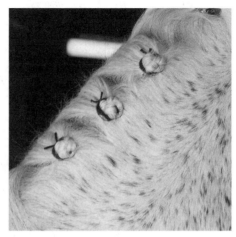

Sewn-in (button) braids. 1) Waxed braiding thread braided into mane and tied at the end. 2)Thread stitched up through the base of the braid and stitched up and down. 3) Finished braid.

A completed row of sewn-in braids.

take the thread and needle around to the right of the braid, then up through the whole braid to the center of the top side again. Now go around the left side of the braid and make a stitch up through it. If needed, repeat to the right and left to secure the braid. Now unthread the needle and cross the ends of the thread underneath the braid, and tie them with a surgeon's knot on the top of the base of the braid. Snip off the ends of the thread.

TAILS

Here's another trick I learned in Germany. Take a very clean, tangle-free tail and braid the skirt (the part hanging below the tail bone) into five to eight long braids, depending on the thickness of the tail, and tie the braids off with a rubber band. Before you compete, unbraid the tail and brush it out with a soft bristled brush or people hair brush. The braiding makes the tail appear very full and floaty, which for some reason seems to enhance your horse's movement. But be careful: if you try this with a dirty or greasy mane (for example, if you didn't wash out the conditioner well enough), your horse will look like he has a bad perm in his limp, lifeless tail. This tail trick works the best on horses that have voluminous tails to begin with, but it will improve the appearance of thin tails as well. I particularly like it because the tail stays cleaner. Iinstead of needing to pick manure, shavings, or pieces of straw out of the whole tail the next morning (and you will invariably miss a few, which will make an appearance right as you go in the ring), you simply dust off each braid and brush the hair out—there is no place for the shavings or straw to hide!

If you are competing in the hunter classes, you will probably also need to braid your horse's tail for the show ring. This involves a tiny French braid down the tailbone which will set off your horse's hindquarters, much as pulling the tail will for eventers, jumpers, and dressage horses. Since I don't braid tails frequently anymore, I'll refer you to Susan Harris' *Grooming to Win*, which has excellent step-by-step illustrated instructions for tail braiding.

WHICH BRAIDS TO USE WHEN

I've already suggested that hunter braids aren't only for hunters. The following is a guideline for appropriate braids in various circumstances. I follow two general rules of thumb, which are sometimes contradictory, although you can usually strike a compromise between the two:

1. *When in Rome.* Braid your horse in the style most prevalent and widely accepted in your sport.

2. *Whatever is best for your horse.* Along this line of thinking, you braid in the style that is most appropriate for your horse given his breed and conformation. So if you are showing in dressage and have an Andalusian or an Arab, you do a French braid along the length of the neck, if you have a Thoroughbred, you do hunter braids, if you have a warmblood, you do European braids.

And now here's the spectrum of what is generally considered "accepted" in each discipline.

DRESSAGE SHOWS

Hunter Braids

I think hunter braids are the only universally accepted braiding style, so if in doubt, do these. They look nice on almost any horse, and they stay in securely. At dressage shows you can choose to accent the braid with white tape wrapped around the braid at and just below the knot in the yarn. Dressage specialty stores have braiding tape, but I also use Johnson's and Johnson's first aid tape (one-quarter inch); it's waterproof, sturdy, and much more economical than braiding tape. The white contrast on the mane will draw attention to the neck, so only tape your braids if the horse has a reasonably nice neck and remains consistently steady in his connection with the bit. It helps if the braids are tidy too—tape can draw unwelcome attention to messy braids.

European Braids

These are appropriate for dressage shows, but they look best on well-muscled necks, particularly on warmbloods. I did use them sometimes on Steel, my Thoroughbred, but I found the hunter braids to be more flattering to his slender neck. Use contrasting white rubber bands to draw subtle attention to the topline; otherwise use matching bands. You can also tape over the bands on these braids. They do not last as long as other braids done with yarn or thread, but they are easily repaired so they can be left in all weekend if your horse is agreeable.

French Braids

Use a French braid only on a horse whose breed has a tradition of allowing the mane to grow long, such as a Friesian, Andalusian, Lusitano, or Arabian. They should not be used on warmbloods or Thoroughbreds, which traditionally have pulled manes. French braids must be put in and taken out daily because they will loosen and buckle as the horse moves around. This is usually not too much of a problem, as this type of braid goes in much more quickly than other braiding styles.

EVENTING

Sewn-in Braids

Due to the British influence on eventing fashion, sewn-in braids are the most fashionable braids for events. Although many people in this country unbraid for cross country so they can grab mane to steady themselves over jumps, braids left in make the horse and rider look very sharp for this phase. In fact, you can leave these in all weekend, as they are among the sturdiest braids.

Hunter Braids

These braids are also totally appropriate for events. You can put the mane up in fewer, larger braids than you would for a hunter show. But don't use white tape on the braids as you might for a dressage show—no one uses white tape at events, even for the dressage phase, no matter how nice the horse's topline is!

For Cross-Country

Even if you plan to unbraid the rest of the mane after dressage, leave the top (first) one in. Untie the braid so that it looks like it did just before you pulled it through: a braided section tied off with a slipknot with two ends of yarn or thread at the end. When you're tacking up for cross-country, securely tie the braid to the crownpiece of the bridle using a surgeon's knot (see the earlier section on hunter braiding). If you and your horse unexpectedly part company on cross-country, the braid will help keep the bridle from getting pulled off, which will make it easier to catch the horse should he run away, allowing you to remount and finish the course with less time lost rearranging your tack.

SHOW JUMPING

Hunter Braids

Again, these braids are appropriate. Use lots of little braids as you would for turning out a hunter. But unlike the hunter, you may choose to leave the forelock loose with hunter braids on a jumper.

European Braids

With the increased importation of European sporthorses, European style turnout is gaining popularity in the jumper ring. If you choose to do these braids, be sure to bang the tail (and pull or trim it if you want) to complete the look.

HUNTERS

Hunter Braids

These are the only braids that are appropriate for an open hunter show. Period. Do not use any other braids! Ever! The only time you might use braids other than hunter braids on a hunter is at a breed show with hunter classes; for example, at an Arabian show, an Arabian hunter could go in a French braid. But if you are at an open hunter show, you had better have that Arabian pulled and braided like a hunter. In a discipline that places such an emphasis on tradition and style, it is important to have the horse's mane braided according to prevailing conventions. Plus, the tail should be braided to complete the picture—see Susan Harris' *Grooming to Win* for instructions.

CLIPPING

I view clipping as a necessary evil. I don't particularly like the idea of robbing my horse of his own natural warm, waterproof winter coat and replacing it with a synthetic one that probably doesn't do as good a job, but if I were to ride him in the winter with that woolly mammoth coat, he would sweat up a storm and easily get chilled in the cold, damp air. So I clip.

I'm not going to give a detailed "how-to" on clipping here; instead I'll refer you to Susan Harris' *Grooming to Win* which does an excellent job of explaining the different clips. But I do have a few helpful hints for you first-time clippers (and maybe for you old campaigners, too!).

First, let's discuss the clippers. I have body clipped entire horses using Oster A5's. They can do the job on fine-coated horses, but they were really meant for heavy-duty trimming or for clipping smaller animals such as dogs. If you're going to body clip, get clippers made specifically for body clipping. It will go faster and be easier on you and the equipment. When I used A5's I had to go slowly and clip one horse over a couple days or the motor would give out. Oster Stewarts are the old standbys; I have clipped many a horse with them and they work very well. However, they vibrate a lot and they are noisy, plus they are heavy so that you (the person doing

Groomer's Edge body clippers.

the clipping) will tire more easily. Also, they are so big that they can be hard to maneuver in certain places; parts of the leg, for example, or the head. Last year I bought a Groomer's Edge wall-mounted 501 model. The motor is separate from the part of the clipper that goes in your hand, resulting in a quiet, lightweight, completely maneuverable handpiece. You just hang the big motor on the wall and off you go with the rest of it. And you can use a normal-sized blade, which is cheaper to buy than the huge ones; I used the #10 blade from my A5's. With any clippers you buy, be sure to read and keep the instructions for use and maintenance. Keep your clippers properly cleaned and oiled as per the manufacturer's instructions and you will extend their life, which is important with such an expensive investment. Also remember to get your blades resharpened, usually after every couple of horses. Look in the yellow pages under *clippers* or if you can't find anything there, call a dog grooming salon and ask them where they take their blades.

GRADUAL FAMILIARIZATION

So now you've got these snazzy clippers...what about the horse? When I faced the task of body clipping Donovan in the fall of his three-year-old year, I considered my options. He had never seen clippers before, so I knew I couldn't just sashay in and start clipping away—it wouldn't be safe for either horse or handler. I didn't want to be forced to rely on the help of a second person to twitch him or hold him for me. I could have tranquilized him and just done it, but then I'd have to tranq him again the next time, and the next time, and I'd have to hurry so I'd get done before the drugs wore off, and he'd probably feel a bit uncertain and concerned about the whole procedure, if not downright scared. The option I ultimately chose took longer, but it paid off in the long run since now Donovan is completely at ease with clipping The technique is based on a general training tool: When introducing a horse to anything new or when resolving his fear or disobedience based on prior bad experience, it is useful to break down a process into small parts and introduce those parts gradually over time.

1. First, I took out my clippers and let Donovan look at them and sniff them and even lick them so he would see that they weren't scary. At first he snorted and was worried, but I spoke to him soothingly and encouraged him to sniff them and he eventually decided they were all right. I gave him sugar and told him he was a good boy. This took place in his stall where he felt

safe (the door was unlatched for my safety), but was enclosed so he couldn't decide to leave just because he was scared—he had to stay and deal with the issue until it was no longer worrisome. As we would for the following steps, we repeated this for several days (complete with treats, pats, and soothing words) until the clippers by themselves were no longer exciting, but instead a positive experience. Donovan is always happy to get a treat! That told me he was ready for the next step.

2. While talking quietly to him, I touched him with clippers all over his body so he could get used to the feel of them. Again this was scary at first, but I didn't make a big deal of it and I wasn't in a hurry, so after a couple of minutes Donovan decided he would survive. Then followed more sugar, more praise, then I repeated for a few days until the whole process became boring.

3. Next I showed him the clippers, by now old hat. Then I plugged them in and turned them on. I stood where he could see and hear them, but I wasn't in his personal space. I talked soothingly to him; then I left the clippers hanging on the wall, turned on so that they were making noise, and patted him and stroked his whole body. He found this phase frightening at first,

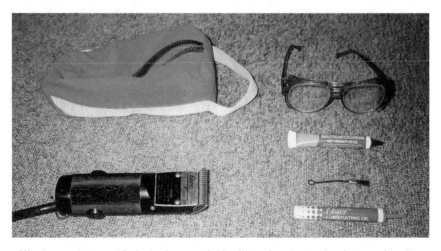

Clipping equipment (clockwise from top left): clipper bag, protective shop goggles, clipper grease, brush for cleaning, lubricating oil, Oster A5 with #10 blades.

and it took several days before he stopped worrying about the noise. I kept giving him sugar and telling him he was a good boy. Again, I wanted him to think of the clippers as a positive experience.

4. Once the horse didn't care about the noise anymore, I started to pat and stroke him while holding the running clippers. I moved the noisy clippers all around his body, but I didn't touch him with them. At the end of the session I clipped a little strip off his shoulder, then told him how brave he was and rewarded him with sugar. We had a few more of these sessions.

WHAT TO WEAR WHILE CLIPPING

This may seem like an odd topic to write about, but I consider it rather important. Novices don't always realize (I sure didn't) that clipping is a messy, yucky job. It's like shedding season but worse; not only is there horse hair everywhere, but it's also blown at you by the fan on your clippers, and it has a very sharp, newly cut edge that will gouge you mercilessly. So wear:

A "slippery" jacket such as Gore-Tex or other raincoat material, as your outermost layer. The hair will slip off the jacket instead of embedding itself into the material, as it will do with sweatshirts. No matter how many times you wash that sweatshirt, you would still be pricked by little flecks of horse hair, believe me. (You can, however, wear sweatshirts underneath that slick outer layer for warmth.)

Silk thermal underwear as your innermost layer. If any hair does get through your Gore-Tex barrier, it will also slip off this layer instead of gouging you.

A surgical mask. Yes, you'll look like a dweeb, but inhaling flying horse hair, dander, and dirt never did anyone any good.

Shop goggles. These nicely add to the dweeb look. I used to go home after clipping, wondering why my eyes were burning, only to look in the mirror and find minute specks of clipped hair inside my eyelids. Ouch! If this happens to you, use a drop of saline eye solution such as Artificial Tears or Alcon Tears Naturale II, and you will blink them out. But, as they say, an ounce of prevention....I started using shop goggles. I suggest the kind that are like eyeglasses with extra shields on the sides and top; the scuba mask kind aren't as comfortable because they don't breathe well and can get clammy and fogged up.

5. Finally we were ready to clip. I put him in the crossties, showed him the clippers, turned them on, and he stood still, happy and relaxed, while I body clipped him. I have to admit he got fidgety a couple of times, but that was due more to being a three-year old that couldn't stand still for too long than it was to his being worried about anything that was going on. Because I had deconstructed the process of getting clipped into smaller, less threatening pieces, he was prepared to deal with the whole shebang when I put it together. He understood what was happening and wasn't scared or worried about it. This method may seem long and drawn-out, and it likely will be with a horse as green as Donovan. Using these same steps, an older, more experienced horse could probably be acclimatized to the clippers in a day or two. Tranquilization would have been a short-term solution, but this method will serve you well over the long run.

WHICH CLIP?

Now that you're all dressed up and ready to go, you can start clipping. If your horse objects to the noise, try loosely stuffing practical cotton in his ears so he can't hear as well. If he's still upset, reintroduce the clippers to him using the method outlined above, or restrain him (see the earlier methods of restraint).

When you choose your clip, take into account what the horse will be doing. Will he be living and working indoors for the winter? Will he be going to Florida or southern California or one of the other winter dressage or hunter/jumper circuits? If this is the case, you can do a full body clip which will make him look nicer for the show ring. Or will he still be getting turned out in the snow? Is he going to be foxhunting or eventing in cool or cold weather? If so, use a hunter clip. The hunter clip leaves hair on part of the face and on the legs for protection, as well as underneath the saddle (I like to leave a patch of hair under the saddle even on full body clips).

If you won't be competing at all and the horse will only be in light work, you can do a trace clip, a blanket clip, or a strip clip, which leave the horse with more of his natural coat. A trace clip removes hair from the lower half of the neck, hindquarters, and barrel, leaving hair on the legs, the upper part of the body, and sometimes the head. A blanket clip leaves the legs and a blanket-shaped patch of hair covering the back and hindquarters but removes the hair from the belly, chest, and neck. A strip clip leaves the most coat of all: it only involves clipping a strip on the underside of the neck, the chest, and belly. Trace, blanket, and strip clips, however, are not appropriate for competition.

Take a realistic look at your own riding habits too: Do you tend to be a "fair weather" rider and let things slide a little in the cold winter months? If you're not going to be riding, consider

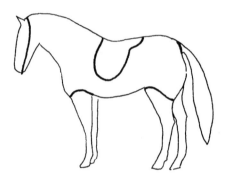

Hunter

Trace

Blanket

Strip

leaving your horse's winter coat as it is. Mother Nature put it there for a reason, so unless you absolutely have to take some or all of it away, don't!

One more thing: whichever body clip you decide on, plan to do it at least a week before you take your horse to the show in question. He won't grow out enough to get too hot in a week, but he will have outgrown that "just shorn" look that he'll have right after you clip him. A few days will soften the clip a little, making it look more natural, and will give him a chance to regenerate the oils in his skin that give his coat its natural shine.

DON'T BUG ME! DEALING WITH INSECTS

I'm a do-it-yourselfer when it comes to my horses, so it makes sense that I make my own fly spray. There are numerous homemade fly spray recipes available on the internet; just go to Google and type in "fly spray recipe" and you will find lots of sites to visit. My favorite fly spray is a variation on a recipe shared with me by another boarder at the barn I was at in high school. The smell is pleasant (to people, not flies!), and it is probably safer than many other fly sprays out there. It is particularly good for horses

FLY SPRAY RECIPE

3 cups apple cider vinegar
3 cups Avon Skin-So-Soft (look in the phonebook under Avon or at www.avon.com)
2 cups water
2 teaspoons* citronella oil (you can buy this at pharmacies)
   *Make sure to use a non-cooking teaspoon—citronella oil is very strong and will not wash off your teaspoon any time soon!

Mix together in a washed out gallon or half-gallon jug, then pour into labeled spray bottles for use. You must shake before each use—like oil and vinegar, this fly spray will separate.

that have skin or respiratory allergic reactions to commercial chemical fly sprays. However, it must be reapplied frequently since it doesn't last long.

TICKS

My fly spray recipe also repels ticks (and fleas, for that matter, if you want to use it on your dog or cat). If you live in a tick-endemic area, spray the skirt of your horse's tail and his legs with Show Sheen before going out of the ring during tick season. The Show Sheen makes the horse's hair more slippery, so it is more difficult for ticks to climb aboard. Check your horse (and yourself!) carefully for the little critters after riding out on the trail, especially if you've gone under trees or through grass. Ticks are likely to be on your horse's legs, tailbone, and mane at the crest. Ticks burrow their heads beneath the skin of their hosts. Although it is tempting to simply pull a tick off your horse, this could result in the body breaking off and the head left behind, which can lead to infection. The better option is to douse a cotton ball in rubbing alcohol and press it against the horse's skin for a couple minutes, covering the tick with the cotton ball. The alcohol will kill the tick (you will notice that the legs stop wiggling) and you can pull the dead tick out easily, head included. It is also wise to handle ticks with latex gloves to prevent contracting Lyme disease or other diseases ticks may carry.

MORE EXTERNAL INSECT CONTROL

A fly sheet will help keep your horse from being eaten alive when he's not being ridden. My favorite fly sheets for fit, comfort, and durability are the Saratoga Oasis fly sheet and the Rambo DustBuster, both of which are designed for turnout but are also an excellent choice for stall wear for horses that are hard on their clothes. In addition, the sheets also offer UV protection. Fly masks

Insect protection for turnout includes fly mask and fly sheet.

are another weapon in my arsenal; my favorite is the Absorbine Ultrashield fly bonnet. If flies flock to your horse's legs, Velcro on a set of scrim leg protectors. When you're riding, you can use crocheted ear nets to keep insects out of your horse's ears and off his face. These ear nets are very popular in the jumper ring, but they aren't allowed for competition in any of the other disciplines except when specially waived in due to unusually buggy conditions.

INTERNAL INSECT CONTROL

Try feeding one-quarter cup apple cider vinegar daily. This is supposed to raise the blood acid level, thereby making your horse less yummy to flies, ticks, and mosquitoes. Most horses like the taste of cider vinegar, so it shouldn't be a problem to feed dressed over grain. Another option to make your horse less tasty is garlic, which purportedly causes sulfur to be excreted through the skin. You can get garlic capsules from the drugstore or the health food store. Break open the capsules and mix with your horse's grain.

YES, WE EAT NO BANANAS

An anthropology professor of mine once described to us the socioecological problem of growing bananas. Because insects love bananas so much, extremely harsh pesticides are needed to grow them, resulting in both contamination of the ecosystem and health problems such as high rates of cancer in those who work in banana fields. The entomological affinity for bananas doesn't stop in the field, however; eating bananas will make you tastier to mosquitoes and other biting insects. So refraining from eating bananas (and refraining from feeding them to your horse) during insect season may help keep the insects at bay.

THE
TACK

Selection of Equipment • Care of Tack

SELECTION OF EQUIPMENT

QUALITY

When choosing tack, it is generally best to buy the highest quality possible. Although inexpensive items may seem enticing at first, they are usually lacking in durability and must be replaced frequently, thus making them more expensive in the long run than better quality goods with a higher price tag. So not only is it safer to ride with more durable tack since it is less likely to break, it is more cost effective as well. German, Swiss, English, and French leather and craftsmanship are traditionally among the best, although the United States and Canada now produce some tack of very good quality. Leather goods from India, Pakistan, Eastern Europe, and Argentina are usually lower in quality, although I believe that it is usually the leather that is the problem rather than the craftsmanship. I have a bridle crafted in India from English bridle leather that I like quite well.

Good quality leather is usually thicker and more consistent in its thickness than its cheaper counterpart. Although blemishes are often present on any piece of leather no matter how high the quality, they should not be unsightly nor should they compromise the product's integrity. Quality leather is firm but pliable in its unbroken-in state, but cheap leather may be either stiff or floppy. Most good leather is coated with a thin layer of whitish wax to protect it during shipping and initial storage, but this coating should be removed prior to use (see tack cleaning). Good leather will also have more stitches per inch than cheaper leather. If you are buying by catalog or over the internet, make sure you either know that the brand is a good one or that the company's policy allows for returns (the item must be unused, of course). If in doubt about the quality of a piece of tack, enlist the help of the tack store salesperson or a knowledgeable friend or instructor.

SYNTHETIC TACK

I once bought a synthetic bridle for daily use because the idea of a bridle that I could clean by running it under a hose was tempting. However, I was less than pleased with it. Whereas leather will become more supple with use and conditioning, that synthetic bridle was stiff when I bought it and it remained so—synthetics do not break in. I have also ridden in some synthetic saddles. I didn't dislike those as much as I did the bridle, but leather gives a much more personalized and comfortable feel because it molds to the shape of the horse and rider. Additionally, a synthetic saddle is not as durable as a high quality leather one.

Another disadvantage of synthetic tack is that it won't break under stress, while leather will. If you absolutely insist on buying synthetic tack, make sure it has breakaway capabilities (e.g., a leather or Velcro insert) should your horse get hung up in the reins or you in a stirrup, and buy it in a conservative color (some version of brown or black, not hot pink or neon green). This advice goes for halters too: A horse can easily get a foot stuck in a nylon halter in turnout, but a leather crownpiece or Velcro attachment point will ensure that the halter breaks before the horse does. Or consider using a halter entirely made of leather; in barn fires, horses that are otherwise safely evacuated can end up with their nylon halters melted into their skin due to the ambient heat, requiring surgical removal!

A conservatively colored synthetic all-purpose saddle.

STYLE

Each discipline will have its own rules, most of them unwritten, about acceptable styles of tack. Unless you have unlimited funds to keep up with all the trends and unlimited time and patience to keep breaking in new tack, it is best to choose conservative, classic styles of tack, particularly with costly items such as saddles. Black tack will probably always be appropriate for dressage. Havana brown tack will probably always be appropriate for jumping. White padded bridles, fancy stitched nosebands, flashy browbands, Newmarket or London colored leatherwork, and other such styles will tend to go in and out. However, with smaller purchases such as saddle pads, you can often afford to follow the styles a bit more; once the fashion has passed, you can always use last year's must-have show pad for schooling at home this year, or it might be worn enough that you need a new one anyway. Other trends tend to fluctuate more slowly, and these you can also follow without breaking the bank; for example, flash nosebands (which help keep the mouth closed) have been "in" in the dressage and event communities for over ten years now. Figure 8s and dropped nosebands serve the same purpose, but it would be rare to see a horse on cross-country with a dropped noseband or in the dressage ring with a figure 8 (although the reverse wouldn't be unthinkable).

SADDLES

The best advice is to find a saddle suitable for your discipline that fits (or can be restuffed to fit) your horse and that you yourself find comfortable. Don't buy a particular saddle because this or that Olympian or World Champion swears by it or because everyone in the barn has one. That celebrity rider could probably ride well on a saddle made of two-by-fours and old suitcases, and not everyone in the barn has the same pelvic width or femur length as you. After you have purchased your saddle, buy a bridle that is the same color and suitable for your chosen discipline or disciplines.

It is easiest to make a sound decision about a saddle if you've sat in a lot of different ones. Tack stores are a good place to do this, and you can enlist the help of the salesperson in determining

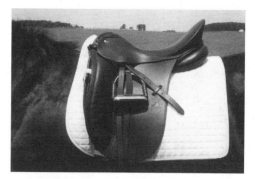

Dressage saddle with a square saddle pad.

how well the different saddles fit you. Once you've narrowed your choices, you can often leave a credit card number with the store and take a saddle home on trial to see if it also fits your horse. Some tack stores will also make "barn calls" and help you fit the saddle to your horse. Even if they don't do such adjustments in-house, most tack stores or your instructor/trainer will probably be able to help you find a qualified saddle fitter.

BRIDLES

Nosebands

The purpose of a dropped noseband is to prevent the horse from evading the bit by opening his mouth. A flash noseband, which combines a caveson noseband and a dropped one, accomplishes the same thing if it fits well. The top part of the flash should be fastened snugly and lie no more than two fingers' width below

Bridle with flash noseband, buckle ends, and loose ring snaffle.

Bridle with figure 8 noseband, hook-stud ends, and brass clincher browband.

the horse's projecting cheekbone. If the noseband doesn't fit, the flash part will pull the caveson part down and neither piece will function. The benefits of flashes is that they can be used with a standing martingale if needed, and that they tend to flatter the horse's face better than would a dropped noseband.

Figure 8s also keep the mouth closed, plus they keep the horse from evading the bit by crossing his jaw. It is thought that figure 8s are less likely to inhibit breathing than flashes or dropped nosebands.

Most dressage riders use padded flash nosebands at the lower levels and the requisite caveson (usually also padded) with the double bridle at the upper levels. I like the currently favored "crank" nosebands, not because I can buckle them super tight, but because they equalize the pressure on the horse's nose and

Padded flash with crank noseband. Crank nosebands can be harsh if overtightened, but used properly they equalize and distribute the pressure on the horse's jaw and decrease stress on the leather at the buckle.

The underside of a padded crank noseband.

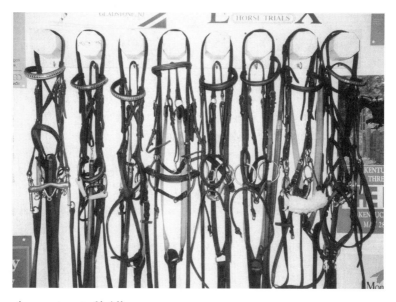

An assortment of bridles.

put less stress on the leather at the buckle than the conventional noseband.

Event riders usually choose either flash or figure 8 nosebands. Jumpers often wear figure 8s or flashes as well. Hunters should go in unpadded caveson nosebands. Dressage horses, eventers, and jumpers often wear decorative browbands, such as brass or silver "clincher" browbands, although plain ones are never incorrect.

Bits

Your instructor or a knowledgeable friend will be able to help you choose the bit that is best for your horse. Use the mildest bit that will get the job done, remembering that (a) any bit in abusive or uneducated hands can be a harsh bit and (b) a bit with enough kick in it to get the job done swiftly is, overall, kinder than the "mild" bit which the rider will be tempted to hang on to or use to nag at the horse. Traditional wisdom tells us that thick bits are gentler, but if your horse has a small mouth, he may not have enough room in there for a big bit to be comfortable and may prefer a thinner bit.

My young horse Donovan did all three phases of events in a loose ring snaffle, as did my previous event horse, Steel. In the dressage ring, a loose ring is the most common bit you will find, although you will also see some eggbutts out there. For upper level horses going in double bridles, the bridoon will usually be a loose ring. Loose rings tend to encourage the horse to mouth the bit, which is important in dressage. Hunters prefer the horse to leave the bit alone, and currently in the hunter ring D-ring snaffles are favored, as are Pelhams. A few years ago full cheeks were in vogue. Both full cheeks and D-rings aid the horse in turning and cannot be pulled through the mouth as loose rings can. KK, French link, single jointed, straight bar, and Dr. Bristol are some common types of snaffles. For the jumpers and the cross-country and show jumping phases of events, you will see much more variety in bits. No matter what, check the rulebook to make sure your bit is legal. Dressage bitting rules are most stringent, but

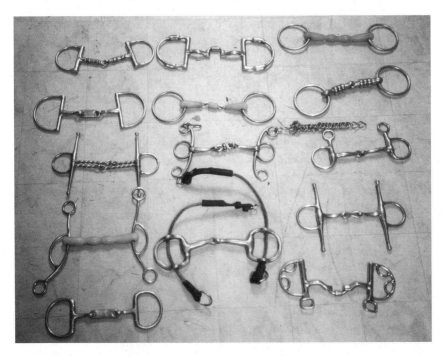

Bits come in many different shapes and sizes.

there are legal and illegal bits in every discipline.

Reins

Hunters usually go in leather reins, braided or laced. Web, web woven with rubber, or plain reins with or without leather stops are common in dressage, although some (myself included) prefer rubber reins. Both jumpers and event riders often favor rubber reins. Rubber reins are especially good with horses that pull because they do not cut into your hands like web ones will. They are also good all-weather reins since they do not become slick in the rain like leather ones.

Both dressage and event reins often have buckle ends rather than hook studs. Buckles are more durable, in addition to currently being fashionable. Eventers, no matter what type of reins are chosen, should knot the reins for cross-country to keep them together should the buckle break and to make them easier to regain if they have slipped over drops.

Top: Plain black leather reins, hook stud ends, no leather stops. Middle: Brown rubber reins. Bottom: Web-rubber reins with leather stops, buckle ends.

Brown braided (plaited) leather reins with hook stud ends are appropriate for the hunter ring.

Martingales

The most common types of martingales used are standing martingales and running martingales. Standing martingales attach to the caveson, and they are often used in the hunters on horses that want to evade the aids by carrying their heads too high. However, in the hunter ring they will also often be used for purely aesthetic purposes: they complete the polished look of a correctly appointed hunter.

Martingales are not allowed in dressage, and eventers may only use running martingales, and these only in the jumping phases. A running martingale is a V-shaped strap with rings on the ends of the V. One rein goes through each ring, sliding freely except near the mouth where the martingale-stop prevents the ring from catching on the bit. The running martingale acts directly on the bit when the horse's head is too high. Jumpers may also use running martingales, but not standing.

Fitting a standing martingale.

You can buy martingales alone or as attachments to breastplates. In either case, try to get your martingale to match your bridle, not just in color but also in style. If your bridle is raised, get a raised martingale. If your bridle is flat, get a flat one. It is important that your martingale fit correctly: too loose and it will be ineffective, too tight and it will prevent your horse from

Fitting a running martingale attached to a breastplate.

using his head and neck properly. Check the fit while the horse is standing still. Run the martingale up the underside of the neck. A running martingale fits when the rings just hit the gullet area where the jaw and neck connect. A standing martingale fits when the strap can run up the underside of the neck to the gullet and then down to the underside of the caveson.

Breastplates/Breastcollars

These pieces of tack keep your saddle from sliding backwards and off the withers. In his book *Training the Three-Day Event Horse and Rider*, Jimmy Wofford does an excellent job describing the function of each. It is uncommon to see "pure dressage" horses in breastplates or breastcollars, but you will see eventers doing dressage in them fairly frequently, as the narrower horses often used for eventing are more prone to having their saddles slip back, particularly as they become fitter in preparation for a three-day. Aesthetically, a breastplate is more flattering to the horse, and it does not inhibit shoulder movement, so of the two, breastplates are more usual in the dressage ring, both for event and dressage horses. Hunters should only wear breastplates, not breastcollars.

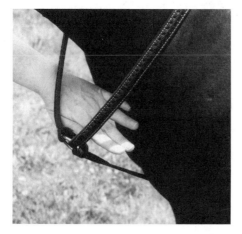

Fitting a breastplate: one hand's width between the center ring of the yoke and the chest.

Breastplate attached to stirrup bars with "dee savers" instead of dee rings.

On the other hand, since breastcollars tend to work better than breastplates, on cross-country events a breastcollar will probably be a better bet. Show jump in either one. One recent trend for eventers for all three phases is sturdy, flat breastplates with multiple points of adjustment and big brass buckles.

Saddle Pads

For saddle pads, hunters prefer shaped, white fleece pads while most of the other disciplines choose square pads (although jumpers may also go in shaped pads). Dressage riders choose square white pads (or cream, especially if their breeches are cream) with a small square or diamond quilt. Some dressage riders will use black pads, particularly on a gray horse, but this is rare. Avoid too large a pad on a small horse—it can be overpowering and make the horse look even smaller.

Jumpers and eventers usually use saddle pads with a larger diamond quilt than dressage pads, and they have more leeway in terms of color choice. However, event riders will usually stay with white or light-colored pads for show jumping and dressage and save the colorful ones for cross-country. Big, thick saddle pads which offer extra protection, such as PolyPads or Rambo pads, are seen on event horses but generally not on show jumpers. Sometimes jumpers and eventers use a shaped fleece pad on top of a square one. Nunn Finer No Slip pads will help keep tack in place if the saddle is prone to sliding, and are used frequently in the event world. If special back-protection pads such as gel pads or sheepskin pads are used, they should be as unobtrusive in appearance as possible. Most back protectors are made to be used between the regular pad and the saddle, but I have a Supracor that is designed to go underneath the regular pad, rendering it invisible.

BOOTS AND BANDAGES

A well-fitting boot or bandage can provide protection against brushing, hitting jumps, or garden variety clumsiness. Bandages, in general, provide more in the way of support for the tendons and ligaments while boots do more for concussion absorption (that is, protection). The one exception is polo wraps, which are basically for protection.

Jumpers often go in open-front leather boots in front and ankle boots behind. This arrangement provides protection from brushing, but will allow the horse to feel if he touches a jump, which is likely to make him more careful. These boots are either neoprene or sheepskin lined. Polo wraps are also acceptable for show jumping.

Eventers go cross-country in a variety of legwear. Leather galloping boots are good protection, but they are more of a hassle to take care of as you can't just throw them in the washer and dryer. Many eventers today like the Porter leg protectors. Apply Vetrap or a Saratoga bandage over the top to keep them in place. There are some heavy duty galloping boots such as the Nunn Finer American Style boots, which are quite popular. Some lower level competitors go in splint boots, and horses with old soft tissue injuries may benefit from sports medicine boots (which are a bear to keep clean if you ride through foxtails or

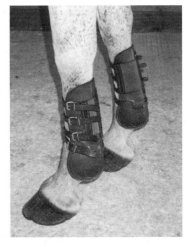

Open front leather jumping boots.

Woof brushing boots.

dry grass). My favorite for ease of use, effectiveness, and cleanability is the old eventing standby, the Woof boot, although it does not protect the front of the ankle like the Porters or the Nunn Finer boots do.

As an added precaution against your boots coming undone, use a spiral of electrical or duct tape over the fasteners. Spiral to avoid forming a continuous band of tape around the leg, since that can restrict the leg and cause injury. Do not use polo wraps for cross-country—they are not secure enough to reliably stay put through the rigors of a cross-country run, and they will absorb water and become a hazard in the water jump.

In addition to boots on the lower legs, you can use bell boots for extra protection across country or on horses that tend to overreach with their hind legs and may yank off a front shoe or injure the heel area. The pull-on variety are the most durable and are generally thought to be the most effective, but they are more difficult to put on and take off than the kind that attach with Velcro. If you go the Velcro route, make sure you buy the double Velcro kind. I like the Pro-Tek brand best.

The rules do not allow you to compete on a dressage horse or a hunter with any kind of boots or bandages except in pas de deux or quadrille classes. But you still may want to use something to protect the legs for warm-up or schooling. Hunters often school in polo wraps, either in their barn colors or in conservative colors such as black, or they wear splint boots or any of the other boots described above. Dressage horses traditionally wear white polo wraps for warm-up and schooling, and also for awards presentations and victory gallops. One might question the practicality of using white on a part of the horse that comes in such close and constant contact with sand and other non-white footing material, but white on the legs makes it easier to see their movement, which can be of assistance when schooling on your own with mirrors or riding in a lesson or clinic. Brushing boots in white or black with fleece on the inside are also a good choice for dressage schooling, but if you go outside the arena with these, they will pick up every burr, prickle, or leaf for miles. Since I do dressage but also go out on trails and event, I use my Woof boots for schooling and keep snow-white polos for awards ceremonies only. I usually warm up for dressage bootless rather than try to remember to remove boots or bandages, which would be especially difficult since I am often competing on my own.

It is critical to learn how to bandage effectively. At best, poor bandaging can fail to do its intended job; at worst, it will seriously injure the horse (for example, causing a bowed tendon). The *USPC Bandaging Guide* is an excellent resource that I still use. Procure the appropriate materials; have a knowledgeable person show you how to do the various types of bandages, including shipping, standing, exercise, polo, figure 8, spider, tail, and others. Practice them so that your skills are ready when a situation requiring a particular bandage arises. You will probably use polo and standing wraps the most frequently.

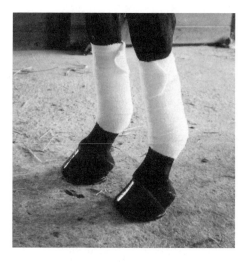

Polo wraps.

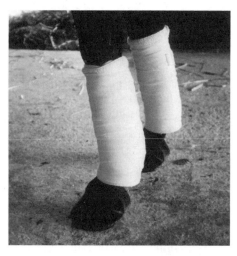

Flannel standing bandages over No-Bow padding.

BUYING USED TACK

There are very few bargains when it comes to horses, but buying your tack used is one of them. I have bought a couple of saddles at a tremendous discount that were "used" (that is, they had left the store and were now owned by someone else) but that hadn't actually *been* used (they hadn't ever even had stirrup leathers on them!). As with new cars, a new saddle loses value as soon as it leaves the store. By buying "new used" saddles, I have been able to get saddles at one-third to one-half off their usual price.

But even buying "used used" saddles can be a good choice, as long as they are in good condition. By good condition, I don't mean that they should look brand new; on the contrary, a saddle will take on more character as it is used. However, there should be no cracked leather, all the billets should be intact, and if there is any loose stitching, it should be in a place where it can be easily repaired. Rest the pommel on your hip and pull the cantle toward you. There should be very little give; if there is more, the tree is probably broken and you should not buy this saddle! Although the lower part of the flap will be more worn than other parts, it should not be paper-thin. Ideally, the leather will have been well cared for, but evaluate whether it is safe and will look and feel nicer after a thorough cleaning and conditioning, or whether it is a completely lost cause. The most important thing in a used saddle is safety.

You could, theoretically, find good used strap goods (bridles, martingales, stirrup leathers, and the like) as well. However, people don't sell these items as frequently as they do saddles, so don't count on being able to find exactly what you are looking for in a used condition. Online auctions such as eBay are an excellent source for bargain used tack. However, be very certain of your size, as items bought on eBay usually can't be returned.

CARE OF TACK

WHY CARE FOR TACK?

If you're like most people, you can probably think of a thousand reasons *not* to clean your tack. You're too busy. It's boring. It just gets dirty again anyway. So it gets cleaned just when you're going to a show...but only the outside of the saddle gets cleaned and you give your show bridle a quick wipe-down while your everyday schooling bridle remains crusty and grungy. There are, however, a few very good reasons why you should clean and condition *all* your tack, not just the part that the judge sees.

SAFETY

All my years in Pony Club have made me a stickler for safety, and that's not a bad thing when you're working with something as big and unpredictable as a horse. If you clean and condition your tack frequently, it is less likely to crack and break at inopportune times (like over a maximum table on cross-country). If there's a bit of stitching that's rotting or coming loose in an obscure place, you are likely to notice that as you clean it so you can have your friend the shoe or tack repairman fix it before it gets out of hand. Conditioning is just as important as cleaning—supple leather will flex where stiff leather would snap.

DURABILITY

Your tack will last longer if it is well cared for. This goes along with the safety point. Many of us ride in sand rings, and even a little bit of sand can quickly eat away at your leather, particularly if the sand is trapped somewhere, such as between your stirrup leathers and saddle flap or along a buckle. Think of what coarse sandpaper would do to your tack—this is what arena sand does to it if left uncleaned. The same goes for stonedust. Oh, and if you ride outside, you're not exempt. Mud and dirt work the same way, and mud has the added ability to dry out your leather and cause cracking, which in turn makes it unsafe.

ADJUSTABILITY

If you do not regularly clean your tack, your buckles and hook studs will have a way of freezing and embedding themselves into the leather so that they are nearly impossible to unbuckle. Not only is this unsafe in the event of an emergency, it can be a hassle if you are using one piece of tack for multiple horses or riders, or if the leather stretches so that you need to adjust the tack to make it fit the same horse over time.

COMFORT

Dirty tack or stiff tack that comes in contact with your horse's coat and skin (such as the bridle and the girth) can cause discomfort, abrasions, and galls (inflamed hair follicles that may make the area swollen, blistered, necrotic, and pus-filled). As for the rider, who wants to hold a pair of rigid reins? Or have stiff saddle skirts digging into your thigh as your instructor torments you with forty-five minutes of sitting trot without stirrups? Ouch!

APPEARANCE

Your tack will look much better if it is clean and supple inside and out. Tack that looks nice reflects well on you as a horseman. Well-cared-for tack develops a rich, mellow luster that cannot be created any other way. Because conditioned tack has resistance to water, you will not have unsightly water spots or discolorations should you get caught in a cloudburst or have a big splash in the water jump.

TIME SAVING

If you clean your tack often, each cleaning takes only a few moments because you will not be removing weeks or months of accumulated grime. So when you do have a big show and you have a thousand other things to do, you will have to spend less time on your tack to make it look show-ring spiffy. I'm the first to admit I don't always get my tack cleaned every single day, but I do try to wipe it down at least every couple of rides, and I take it completely apart for a thorough cleaning and conditioning every few weeks, even when I'm not competing.

I'll step off my soapbox now that (I hope!) I've convinced you why you should clean your tack, and I'll move on to *how* to clean it so that the procedure is as swift and painless as possible.

EVERYDAY CLEANING

If you periodically take your tack completely apart for a thorough cleaning and conditioning, you shouldn't need to do much more than wipe it down with a mild cleanser after each ride or two. If you're short on time, at least rinse off the bit, clean the girth, and sponge off obvious dust, dirt, or sand with saddle soap. Other important areas to hit are the stirrup leathers (including the crease where the iron goes), the part of the flap under your calf, and the noseband and reins of the bridle.

The following recipe produces a concoction that acts as a cleaner, conditioner, and water protectant all at the same time. It is mild enough to use daily, and even though you can rinse it off, you don't really need to since it doesn't tend to build up as much as commercial "all in one" tack care products do. It is much less expensive as well. Consistent use will leave your tack clean and supple. Alternatively, Murphy's Oil Soap, which can be found in liquid and spray forms at grocery stores with the cleaning supplies or at tackstores, can be used as a daily cleanser. However, it should be rinsed well as it tends to build up.

TO THE NINES SADDLESOAP

Ingredients:

1/2 pint half and half (8 oz or 1 cup)

2-3 small bars glycerine soap (about 3.5 oz each)—these can be found at drug stores and bath shops in a variety of colors and scents

Plastic containers (Rubbermaid or Tupperware products, along with disposable alternatives such as Ziploc and Gladware containers, are good choices, although old margarine tubs work just as well)

In a loosely covered microwave-safe container or a 2-quart (medium-sized) saucepan, melt the glycerine with medium low heat, stirring continuously on the stove or several times if microwaving. Once the soap is melted, remove from heat and stir in half and half. Pour mixture into plastic containers and refrigerate until solid. If the kind of glycerine soap you're using is difficult to melt, you can add the half and half and heat that up too to help. With this method, the finished soap may have a pale caramel tinge to it.

To use: Apply to leather with a small, damp tack sponge in an up and down or circular motion. If lather is excessive, rinse sponge and wipe again.

SPECIAL OCCASION TACK CARE

In Pony Club competitions, you are judged not only on your riding but also on your horse management abilities. Before your first ride, there is a "formal inspection," in which a horse management judge scores you on the cleanliness and condition of your tack, your horse, and your own turnout. Unlike the dressage judge sitting at "C" or the hunter hack judge in the middle of the ring, the horse management judge can look underneath your saddle flaps, unbuckle your buckles, and scrape at obscure parts of your tack with his or her fingernails to try to find dirt or residue. I've heard stories of judges a few generations back conducting formal inspections wearing white gloves. That has never happened to me, but I did have one judge who ran her hands all over the tack and the horse and then wiped her hands on a big baby wipe. Part of the score was determined by how much dirt came off on the baby wipe! After formals, you go and warm up, ride your dressage test or jump your course or play your games or whatever, and an hour later you have "turnbacks," another set of cleanliness inspections to show that you have taken care of both your horse and equipment promptly and effectively after your ride. My dad always said he thought Pony Club was a good experience—it was like being in the Marines!

If you are not going through such a militant inspection, there are some suggestions in this section that you will use more frequently than others. But it's good to know about the extremes anyway. You would want your tack to look as nice as possible, for example, if you were selling your saddle or if you were going to an extra-important competition—a three-day event or the regional dressage championships, perhaps.

COMPLETE CLEANING AND CONDITIONING

Every so often, take your tack completely apart to thoroughly clean and condition it. How often depends on the amount of use your tack gets and under what conditions it is used. Do you ride in

CLEANING EQUIPMENT

Small bucket of warm water. Change the water whenever it gets too murky. When traveling or working in a smaller space, I often use a plastic sour cream or ice cream container instead of a bucket. Of course, the water in a smaller container must be changed more frequently.

Small round tack sponges. I used to use the usual colored rectangular kitchen sponges, but tack sponges work much better—they're stronger and you can buy them economically in packs of twelve.

Bar of castile soap. Although there must be others, Kirk's is the only brand I know of. Its label is white with black and red lettering, and it's available at both drug and tack stores.

Soft bristled toothbrush.

Dental pick. These are essential for crevices or stubborn grime.

Dental floss.

Nevr-Dull metal polish (or a similar product—mine is called Everbrite).

Clean rags. You can buy bags of plain cotton, diaper, or terrycloth shop rags at auto parts stores or hardware stores.

Leather conditioner. I used to love a product called Leatherizer, but I have not seen it in several years so I do not know if it is still available. My personal favorite is Passier's Lederbalsam; look for Passier's signature logo. Carr & Day & Martin's Leather Balsam, which comes in a small white tub with a pale blue label, is also excellent. Both these products have beeswax in them, which helps with water resistance (water will bead off your tack instead of soaking in), and although I have tried other leather conditioners with beeswax, I have found these two to be the best. In addition to making it supple, they give your leather a subtle shine that sharpens your presentation in the show ring, and they can be used fairly often without causing the leather to lose its body. I shy away from neatsfoot oil; I was always taught it rots stitching, and whether or not that is true, I do know that frequent use makes leather limp and lifeless, in addition to darkening the color quickly and providing little protection from water. Also, neatsfoot oil used on your saddle will stain your breeches while these other leather conditioners will not.

rain? in an arid climate? in mud? in a sand ring? Does your horse sweat a lot? If you have trouble remembering which holes your cheekpieces, noseband, and stirrups go on, write this information down as you are taking the bridle apart, for example, noseband, third from top; L. cheekpiece, fourth from bottom, and so on.

CLEANING

Wipe away obvious surface dust, dirt, mud, and sand with a damp sponge. (There shouldn't be any dirt if you have been wiping down your tack religiously after riding, right?) Then rub the damp sponge across the castile soap and use the sponge in a circular motion (on the saddle) or an up and down motion (on small straps such as the throatlatch). Pay special attention to stress points such as the hole you always use on your billet straps or the part of your stirrup leathers that bends through your stirrup irons. You may find dirt jockeys, small accumulations of grease and dirt that can erode your leather if left to fester. Gentle but persistent soaping with the sponge is usually enough to eradicate dirt jockeys, but if they are very stubborn, scrub them gently with a castile-soaped toothbrush. Use the toothbrush also to reach crevices on your saddle that are too small to get with the sponge. Castile soap does a better job of removing dirt than does homemade saddlesoap, but it's also harsher, so make sure you rinse your leather well by rinsing the suds out of your sponge and toothbrush and wiping or rubbing all leather surfaces until they are soap-free.

Tack cleaning supplies (clockwise from top left): leather conditioner, metal polish, rag, toothbrush, castile soap, dental picks, Q-tips.

IF YOU WANT TO GET PICKY

Dental picks (your dentist will probably be happy to give you an old one if you so request) are unparalleled for reaching impossible-to-reach places, scouring grime from under the nail on your saddle skirt, and cleaning dirt and soap residue from buckle holes. Keep a paper towel or rag handy to clean the pick frequently. You can also use the dental pick to remove grime on the well-soaped flesh side of the leather itself, but be sure to scrape gently with the flat edge only—the point will scratch the leather. Dental floss is also good for cleaning inaccessible locations on your tack.

METAL CARE

Your leather will still be damp from its cleaning, so while it's drying you can move on to your metal. Some people swear by Brasso metal polish, but I prefer the simplicity of Nevr-Dull. When you open the can, you will see a big chunk of wool that's been soaked in metal polish. Pinch off a bit and, using a circular motion, rub all the metal on your saddle, including the stirrup bar, and all the buckles on your bridle. Do not clean the bit with Nevr-Dull or most other metal polishes; they are usually not safe to ingest and your horse will probably dislike the taste. After a few minutes, use a soft clean rag to buff the metal to a shine. To get a truly super shine, I spend the extra time and use Herm Sprenger Diamond Paste, which is also safe to use on the mouthpieces of bits.

BITS

There are several good ways to clean bits. If you rinse your bit off every time you ride (and you should do this regardless of whether you clean any of your other tack, it takes all of two seconds), it probably won't be too dirty, but it still should be more thoroughly cleaned from time to time.

Dishwasher: Put the bit in the dishwasher along with your dishes, and it will come out nicely cleaned.

Boiling: Bring a small saucepan of water to boil, and drop the bit gently in the boiling water. Leave it for ten minutes or so. Any accumulated grime will loosen and float to the top of the water, leaving the bit clean.

Ultrasonic cleaner: My dad has an ultrasonic cleaner, as does my dentist. This is one of the most effective methods of cleaning bits, but I assume most people don't have such a machine sitting around the house. If you do have access to one, fill it with water, add the bit, and turn it on, leaving it for ten minutes or so. It will literally vibrate tartar, saliva, and old chewed up grass off the bit.

Toothbrush and toothpaste: Some horses are fond of mint, so you can simply brush the bit clean with toothpaste. Be sure to rinse the bit well afterwards.

Herm Sprenger metal polish: this is safe to use on the mouthpiece of bits, according to the manufacturer. Apply as noted on label.

GIRTHS

If your girth has light-colored elastic on it, you can clean the elastic with a toothbrush and toothpaste. Alternately, you can wash the girth in your washing machine with detergent and a little bleach—just make sure to condition the leather properly once it has air-dried enough to absorb the conditioner. I chose my current jumping girth with dark brown elastic to match the leather, so I just clean it with castile soap; I find the matching elastic to be more aesthetically pleasing as well as easier to keep clean.

SUEDE

If you have suede knee rolls or a suede seat on your saddle, you can clean the suede by brushing it gently with medium fine sandpaper. If the suede is really dirty, use a small amount of hand degreaser (found at your auto parts store), and rinse with a damp sponge after several minutes.

STIRRUP PADS

First, pop your stirrup pads out of the irons. Using a toothbrush and castile soap or toothpaste (whitening for white stirrup pads, any kind for black stirrup pads), scrub your stirrup pads. If they are black, you can rinse them right away and leave them on paper towels to drip-dry. If they are white, allow the toothpaste foam to sit on them for ten to fifteen minutes before rinsing. You can also whiten stirrup pads with a bleaching sink cleanser such as Soft Scrub, which works well, or with plain bleach. Bleach, however, tends to break down the rubber.

CONDITIONING

Once your tack is clean and mostly dry (room temperature air-dry only, please—your tack will crack if you leave it in the sun or in front of a heat source to dry), condition it with your chosen leather conditioner. I prefer to apply my leather conditioner with my fingertips because I find it easier to rub in evenly that way. If you'd rather not get your fingers too gooey, use a small tack sponge (*not* the same one you use for cleaning—keep them separate) or a soft rag. Apply lighter coats to the smoother side of your leather and heavier coats to the rougher, flesh side (usually the outside of stirrup leathers, the back side of bridle parts, and the underside of saddle flaps). The flesh side is more porous and can better absorb the conditioner. Allow the tack to sit so the conditioner can soak in, and you're done!

BREAKING IN NEW TACK

If you take a piece of new tack straight from the tack store to the barn and ride in it right away, it will be stiff, uncomfortable, and may chafe you and your horse. Its lack of suppleness makes the tack more likely to develop cracks that could have been prevented had it been conditioned before you put it to use.

Most new tack will have a protective coating of whitish wax on it when you buy it. This is to protect the tack during shipping and can be removed with castile or homemade saddlesoap. You can condition the tack right away with the same leather conditioners you have for tack that is already in use, but the breaking-in process will be a bit slower that way. I like to use olive oil on brand-new tack: It absorbs easily, it won't harm the stitching, the color stays relatively unchanged, and it helps the tack become more supple. Use only olive oil, as other vegetable oils such as corn or canola may go rancid after application. You can buy a big, store-brand bottle fairly inexpensively at the supermarket—you do not need to use gourmet extra extra extra virgin olive oil imported from Tuscany for breaking in your new tack!

Olive oil is especially good on strap goods such as bridles and stirrup leathers, but for a saddle, you should only use it on the underside of the saddle flaps and skirts. If you use it on the outside of your saddle, it will stain your breeches. Olive oil can be applied with a rag or a small paintbrush, which is especially useful on saddles. Fold the leather back and forth, rolling it in your hands to help it absorb the oil and become more supple. One or two applications of olive oil should be sufficient for strap goods; do not use olive oil as your principal long-term conditioner or your leather will lose its body and become limp. Saddles, however, may be olive-oiled daily on the flesh side of the leather for a couple of weeks, which will greatly facilitate the breaking-in process. Oil the outside of your saddle with the leather balsam conditioners noted in the previous section. Always make sure your tack is clean before you condition it.

AGH! IT'S ALIVE: NEGLECTED TACK

How to reclaim neglected tack depends in part on where it was stored while unused. In drier regions, like California where I grew up, neglected tack put away clean became dry and dusty, so all it needed was a good cleaning and conditioning. The only time I saw moldy tack was when I left a flash strap in my trailer over the winter and the roof leaked—the result was a very green and fuzzy flash in the spring! In more humid regions such as the South and the East Coast, tack will go moldy if left unused in the tackroom or even in closets in your house.

To get rid of mold, I use apple cider vinegar applied with a soft rag or tack sponge. Clean the sponge and dampen it with water, and then wipe the tack again to rinse the vinegar off. Allow the tack to air-dry in a well-ventilated area to preclude re-molding, and then condition as usual. If the tack has been put away very, very dirty (perish the thought!), conventional cleaning methods may not be sufficient to truly get it clean. If the piece in question is a bridle, girth, martingale, or the like, you can submerge it completely in a bucket of warm (not hot!) castile-soapy water. Swish it around, rub it with a sponge to loosen the crusted mud and dirt, and allow it to soak ten to fifteen minutes. Then swish it around again and dunk it in a bucket of clean warm water to rinse. Allow at least a day for it to air-dry completely, and oil it several times during the drying process, allowing the conditioner to soak in between each treatment. This type of cleaning is recommended only for extremely dirty tack that simply won't come clean with "spot cleaning." Even though you condition the tack well at the end, it is a fairly harsh method and so shouldn't be used regularly but only as a last-ditch alternative.

TACK STORAGE

If you know you won't be using your tack for an extended period of time, clean it well before storing it. Take your stirrups off your saddle and hang the leathers by the buckles up on a wall. Put a saddle cover on your saddle and keep it on a saddle stand or rack (or something similarly shaped—my show jumping saddle, which didn't fit Donovan, has lived on the back of one of my upholstered kitchen chairs for about two years). If possible, don't hang your bridle on a

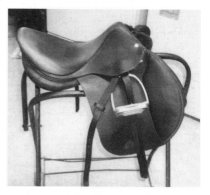

Saddle racks allow saddles to rest in a natural position in storage.

nail; instead, get a bridle bracket, which allows your crownpiece to lie in a more natural position. You can also make your own bridle brackets by nailing old boot polish, tuna, or saddle soap tins to a hanging two-by-four board or directly to the wall, and then painting them in your barn colors to make them snazzy. Always store your tack in a well-ventilated area; this can be a spare room in the house, the tack room if it's climate-controlled, your finished basement if you have one, or your garage if you live in a temperate climate.

TACK REPAIR, OR "MY HERO, THE SHOE REPAIR GUY"

No matter how well you care for your tack, it will need some repair from time to time. If you are vigilant, you will be able to catch rotting or loose stitching and have the item restitched before the situation deteriorates and you find yourself with a broken stirrup leather while jumping a course. If you have access to a tack repair shop, great. Most of us don't. However, shoe repair people

*A tack hook hanging near the sink
makes for convenient tack care.*

are easy to find, and they can often do a fantastic job with tack! (I have never taken a pair of shoes to a shoe repair shop, but I have given my local shoe repair store plenty of business nonetheless!) Restitching, attaching a nameplate, and moving buckles to shorten too-long cheekpieces and nosebands are all ways in which our shoe repair guys help us. Like your auto parts store, the shoe repair shop is a great, non-horsey resource for your horsey needs.

THE
SHOW

Prepare to Compete • Final Words • Helpful Lists

PREPARE TO COMPETE

THE PAPER CHASE

It's showtime! Well, almost showtime. It's a couple months before that, and you're sitting with your omnibus or prize list looking lost. Navigating all the paperwork needed to get you to a show may be a daunting task, but it can be made relatively swift and painless with a little organization beforehand.

MEMBERSHIP

First and foremost, make sure that you are a member of all the appropriate organizations: USDF (United States Dressage Federation), USEF (United States Equestrian Federation, formerly USAEquestrian, and before that, American Horse Shows Association), USEA (United States Eventing Association), NHJA (National Hunter Jumper Association), and smaller local organizations are some that might apply. Some organizations allow you to compete if you pay a nonmember fee, but usually if you plan to show more than a couple of times in a year the nonmember fees add up to more than the membership would have cost in the first place. USEF also requires you to choose at least one breed or discipline affiliation. If you choose one discipline and decide to compete in another, you will have to pay a discipline fee for the other discipline at that show. There is a platinum membership which gives you access to all disciplines; I am an eventing member, which means I can show in eventing, dressage, and jumper competitions as long as I am also a member of USEA.

There are other practical reasons to join the appropriate organizations: Nonmember scores may not count toward year-end or cumulative awards; such is the case with USDF. Even worse, a nonmember entry may not be accepted if there are more entries than spaces available in the competition. (USEA events give priority to USEA members; this applies only to beginner novice since membership is required for novice and above.) In addition to competitive benefits, many organizations offer educational opportunities for their members, such as USDF adult camps and USEA clinics, as well as magazines or newsletters that keep members abreast of the various goings-on.

For some disciplines and levels of competition, you are required to have your horse recorded or registered as well. Usually

SOME MEMBERSHIP AND FEE REQUIREMENTS

To give you an idea of what might be required, consider several examples from my own experience:

- **USDF/USEF dressage show in California:** Requires USEF membership or nonmembership fee for rider, owner, trainer, and (if applicable) coach; and CDS (California Dressage Society) membership or nonmembership fee for rider and owner. Horse must have an HID or be recorded with USDF and USEF.

- **USDF Regional Championships qualifying class:** Requires USEF membership for rider, owner, trainer, and (if applicable) coach; USDF participating membership (careful—this is different from group membership!) for rider and owner; USEF horse recording; USDF horse registration (HID numbers do not qualify.)

- **USEA event, training level:** Requires USEA membership for rider; USEA 4novice/training level horse registration.

- **USEA event, preliminary level:** Requires USEA membership for rider; USEA horse registration (different class of registration for prelim and above); USEF membership or nonmembership fee for rider, owner, trainer, and (if applicable) coach.

Note: USEF's definition of "trainer" is simply the adult on the grounds responsible for the horse. If your "real" trainer won't be at the show and you are over eighteen, you can sign that yourself; juniors may have parents sign without the parent having to pay a nonmember fee. I always sign myself as trainer, no matter what, to expedite the entry paperwork process. If anyone will be coaching you or warming you up while at the show, regardless of whether they're getting paid to do it, that person must sign your entry in the space for "coach" and be a member of USEF or pay the appropriate nonmember fees. Unlike the "trainer" box, which must have a signature even if it's the same person who signed as owner or rider, the "coach" box need not be signed if no one is going to coach you.

this is done on a lifetime basis, so unlike your membership, it will not have to be renewed annually. (USEF, however, does offer an annual horse recording, but two years of that costs more than the lifetime fee.) If you are not competing at a level which requires your horse to be registered, both USEF and USDF require you to have a horse identification number (HID). As of 2005, there is no fee for a USEF HID and a small fee for a USDF HID which can later be applied to the recording fee. All horses competing at USEF or USDF competitions are required to have an HID or a registration number. However, you don't need two HID numbers: USEF will accept your USDF HID, and the two organizations are working on consolidating their systems.

There are certainly many different permutations of registration and membership requirements. The best thing to do is to assess before the beginning of the competition year which types of competitions you plan to participate in and read the prize lists, omnibus entries, and entry forms to determine what is required. Be sure to join *early* so that you receive all your membership cards in time. Otherwise, for a USEF membership for example, you may have to sign an affidavit at the show and pay a fee if you cannot produce your membership card or a facsimile of it. Most of the organizations allow you to pay your membership online and print a verification or temporary membership card.

COGGINS TESTS

Another piece of paperwork you can and should get out of the way early on is your Coggins test. The Coggins test is for equine infectious anemia, a disease that has no vaccination, treatment, or cure and can be fatal (and in some states, horses with EIA must by law be destroyed). Your vet will pull a blood sample from the horse and send it to a lab to be tested, and you will be sent the results. Make sure to use the same name for your horse on the Coggins as you will for entering the competition; that is, don't use his "barn name" on the Coggins if he has a different "show name."

Most shows require a negative Coggins within twelve months of the show date; some require one within six months; some require none at all. Requirements will vary geographically due to the relative threat of EIA. In California, Coggins usually are required for out-of-state horses only. In Tennessee, Coggins usually are required for trailering in for lessons or riding on public facilities. Even if only one of your shows in the year requires a Coggins, make sure to get the test done early each year since it may take several weeks to get the results back. And be sure that you always have a copy of your horse's Coggins test with him when he's traveling, even if you're not headed for a competition; in some states (e.g., Virginia), if a horse is in transport without a valid Coggins, the horse, truck, and trailer can be impounded!

COPIES

Once you have all your necessary membership cards and other paperwork in hand, make copies! USEF recognized shows always require copies of that card, and other organizations may require theirs too. If you are an "eventing" member of USEF, you are allowed to compete in dressage and jumper shows without paying additional discipline fees, but you must have proof of USEA membership. So even though USEA doesn't require copies of cards at events, you will need them anyway if you do dressage or jumpers. At the beginning of the year, I arrange all my membership cards so they fit on a single sheet of paper and photocopy as many copies as I think I'll need (one per show), plus a few extra just

Memberships and entry forms and prize lists—oh my!

in case. When I was riding Steel, I put Kim's (Steel's owner) membership cards on that same sheet too. Yes, that means that I'll send some cards where they're not needed—my USDF card to event secretaries, for example—but putting all your cards on one piece of paper simplifies things both for you and for the show secretary. Instead of making individual copies of cards each time it's time to send in an entry, you've made one trip to Kinko's or the office copier and you don't have to think about it again till next year when there are new cards. The show secretary gets all the membership information he or she needs on one page. Plus, if you happen to lose your membership cards sometime during the year, you will always have plenty of copies so you won't have to replace your cards.

So you now have your copies of cards. Make several copies of your horse registrations too. Although these aren't always required—read your prize list to be sure—it's good to have some around anyway. Make copies of your Coggins too. Then find the entry forms you'll use throughout the year. Some shows require you to use their specific entry forms; others publish one in an omnibus that is standard through the country (e.g, USEA) or area (CDS, USDF Region 1). If some or all of your competitions will be using these standard entry forms, fill one out with as much information as you can that will remain constant throughout the year: the horse's name, age, breed, height, etc.; your address and membership numbers; the owner's address and numbers if someone else owns the horse. Do not sign the releases, however; signatures must be originals. Make copies of your partially completed entry forms. Make a few more copies than you think you'll need—you can always use the extras for scratch paper at the end of the year, and it is better to have extras than to accidentally run out. Now all you'll have to do before each show is fill in the specifics: show name and date, divisions and classes, fees, and sign it. Pretty easy, huh?

Do be sure to keep at least one or two completely blank forms around just in case you ride another horse or someone else rides yours.

YOUR SECRET STASH

In your file cabinet or desk, make a folder that says "Entry Paperwork" and put most of the copies there. Put one copy of everything in the glove box of your truck (if you don't trailer yourself to shows, put copies in something that will always accompany you to shows: the front pocket of your garment bag, for example). If you forget to put your cards or Coggins in with your entry, or somehow they are lost or misplaced, you will have the copies in your truck or bag as a backup! I also always keep my USEF Rule Book in the truck or trailer for easy reference, along with copies of the dressage tests for dressage and eventing in case I need a last-minute memory jog.

CHEAT SHEET

Now sit down at your computer and make a list of membership and registration numbers for all applicable associations for the rider, owner, and horse. This may seem redundant since you already have your membership card sheet, but it's not; your sheet will only have membership cards on it, not horse registrations, which are often an entire page themselves. Having all your numbers in one place will make your life much easier, especially when you've got to get your entry postmarked that day and the post office is about to close. I tack my number sheet up on the wall by my desk so I don't have to go searching for it when I do entries—it's always right in front of me. You won't need this if all your shows use a standardized entry form, of course, but there always seems to be one or two that don't.

ALMOST THERE

Look at this—you're completely organized with your paperwork and the show season hasn't even started yet! Well done! Now obtain and read the prize lists or omnibus entries for the shows you plan to enter. Glance over them as soon as you get them so you have a general idea of what's needed; make note of any special qualifications or other requirements. Use a colored highlighter to keep track of pertinent information. When you sit down to do your entry, read everything carefully once more to be sure that you're providing all the information and paying all the fees required, such as drug, number, or office fees. It will take a little extra time, but better now than once you've arrived on the showgrounds and you're running late and have other things to attend to. (Your careful reading of the prize list and completion of the entry form will also make the show secretary's life much easier—it is surprising how many people send in incomplete entries that are big headaches for the secretary!) Some shows charge a fee if your entry is incomplete, others give a rebate if it isn't, still others simply do not accept incomplete entries. The moral of the story? Do your entry completely and accurately the first time! If you read the prize list or omnibus entry closely, it will tell you everything you need to know about how to do this.

TIME IS OF THE ESSENCE

Always send your entry in on opening day, if there is one. Opening day is the first day that your entry may be postmarked. If postmarked before this day, the entry will not be accepted. For USEA events, opening day is the Tuesday six weeks before the event; it will vary for other shows, or there may be none at all. Why enter so early? You will have a much better chance of getting in. Some shows are so well attended that they fill up immediately, and if you send your entry even one or two days later it will not make it.

If you've entered on the opening date and later decide not to compete, you can usually get your entry and stabling fees back as long as you cancel before the closing date. Sometimes you can even get a refund after the closing date if the show secretary can fill your space from the waiting list. There is often a small fee associated with getting your entry refunded, but I consider it a small price to pay given the flexibility it provides you. In effect, you can make your decision about whether or not to go to a particular show much closer to the show date than you'd be able to otherwise. If instead you wait and send your entry in around the closing date, you probably won't get in the show at all.

Information regarding refunds for the specific competition can be found in the prize list or omnibus entry, which of course you've read carefully. Entering early isn't necessary for some shows, however, because they don't tend to be oversubscribed. Talk to your trainer and other riders in the area about which shows you absolutely need to be on time for and which ones you can wait on, keeping in mind that the popularity of a show may vary from year to year depending on what else is on the calendar.

You may have the option of entering some competitions over the internet, using a credit card. When this sort of entry procedure becomes more widespread, you will probably be able to enter the unchanging information (e.g., numbers, addresses, names) just once a year, and with a few clicks of the mouse make all necessary adjustments for each individual show. This will streamline the procedure both on the competitors' end and on the secretaries' end. Some people, however, are still uncomfortable with the idea of using credit cards and

Impeccably groomed dressage horse (USET Festival of Champions).

making important transactions on the internet (what if entry gets lost on the way?), so it is probable that the paper-based system will continue as well, at least for a while.

CHEF D'EQUIPE

When the USET (United States Equestrian Team) takes riders to international competitions to represent our country, they assign a *chef d'equipe* (captain of the team) to make sure that everything goes smoothly. This person is ultimately responsible for all the little details involved in getting horse and rider into the competition arena in the best form possible. It is amazing that a single incorrect, seemingly unimportant detail can adversely affect the whole performance and experience. My advice? Designate your own chef d'equipe! It can be your spouse, parent, teenager, friend, significant other, or even yourself if need be. It doesn't matter who, just as long as there is someone responsible and capable enough to handle the details.

DUTIES

Details

Your chef d'equipe should review the prize list or omnibus entry again to make sure that he or she knows what is involved with that particular competition. Has the rider sent in all the correct fees, paperwork, signatures, and numbers? When may the horse move into the stabling area? It is a real pain to arrive on the showgrounds nice and early and find out you can't move in yet, or to pull in late at night only to realize that you are required to have someone check you in and the gates have been locked for the day. Is bedding provided, available for purchase on the showgrounds, or does the chef need to make sure to bring some from home? How about hay? Are there any briefings or meetings that the rider must attend? When are they?

Lodging

What sort of accommodations will the rider and the rest of the entourage stay at while at the show? If there are hotels listed and you want to stay in one, book a room as soon as you enter the show, if not sooner. Most hotels and motels let you cancel without penalty twenty-four to forty-eight hours before check-in, and horse shows are often held in remote areas with few options for lodging, so what is available tends to fill quickly. There is often a special rate for the show; the prize list will usually specify if this is the case. Once the chef has found accommodations, he or she should circle which one it is in the prize list (I have arrived at shows having forgotten where I had reservations!) and write down any pertinent information alongside confirmation number (very important—motels can lose reservations, resulting in a weekend of sleeping in your trailer!). Include price, configuration (how many beds of what size did you reserve?), address, and directions from the showgrounds. The prize list should go along with you to the show, and then you will have this important information at your fingertips for the weekend.

Directions

If it is a new show for your team and you're not familiar with the area, the chef should obtain a local map and also a map of the route from your home base to the show. Websites such as http//maps.google.com and www.mapquest.com will give door-to-door, turn-by-turn directions that are generally useful. However, it is important to have a backup resource (that is, a paper map) as well. Occasionally these mapping sites will tell you to turn on streets that do not exist, send you on a circuitous or traffic-congested route, or lack important information in their databases about smaller country roads. If you are a member of AAA, you can get almost any map you need for free. Triple A is the

Must-haves for the road: atlas, tour books, maps, cell phone.

bargain of the century, since they will also come bail you out should you have car trouble or a flat tire, but I would join just for the maps alone. Your local office will probably have whatever you need if you're going to a nearby or popular location; if you're going to a more obscure place, they can order maps for you. This usually takes a couple of weeks, so plan ahead! Getting lost on the way to the showgrounds before the crack of dawn when you have a 7 a.m. ride is no fun—be prepared.

Food

It is better not to rely entirely on horse show food for sustenance. A regional guidebook, also free from AAA or the "local" page on google, will contain other suggestions for lodging and restaurants. However, you will probably be quite busy at the show and won't have time to leave the showgrounds for food until the end of the day. Although there are noteworthy exceptions, horse show food is often greasy, overpriced, inconveniently located, unappetizing, and largely devoid of nutritional value. You are an athlete, and you must feed yourself as such. If you do not eat for the whole day, your blood sugar level will drop and you will have lower energy—not good for a demanding sport. A greasy cheeseburger and fries sitting at the pit of your stomach as you begin your ride won't do you any favors either. Have your chef pack a cooler (you can replenish the ice daily from the ice machine at your hotel) with fruit—fruit will give you energy but is light so it won't weigh you down. You can also bring meals from home packed in Tupperware-style containers in your cooler. Pasta salads with plenty of vegetables and a protein source like chicken or tofu tend to travel well. Make sure it's something that tastes reasonably good cold. I also keep a supply of energy bars (protein bars and the like) stashed in my trailer. No, despite what the manufacturers claim, they don't really taste that great, but they will keep you alive and do more for you nutritionally than french fries would. And always be sure to eat breakfast, even if it's just a banana or a Nutrigrain bar. You are going to be working yourself hard throughout the day, and you can't go around running on empty—you will crash.

Fluids

Even more important than food is water. At some shows I've attended, the water sources all said "nonpotable" or "not for human consumption." Although this made me nervous about what I was providing for my horse, I was grateful that I always bring my own water to shows. Then it's always there, I don't have to go looking for it, I know I won't run out, and it tastes good. If you like, you can also supplement with a sports drink such as Gatorade. When I once got heat exhaustion and mild dehydration at a show, Gatorade helped keep me functional. I was weak, dizzy, irritable, and lightheaded, and I couldn't think clearly. My leg muscles cramped, and I was nauseous. Although it was very hot and humid, I felt chilled, and I was insatiably thirsty. When you have lost enough electrolytes through sweat, simple water will not hydrate you—you can drink and drink and not feel any less thirsty. You must replace the electrolytes, which I did by eating table salt out of my hand and drinking Gatorade. The chef should ensure that there will be enough fluids for the rider and other people in the party (family, friends, etc.) during the show. About a gallon a day per person is usually sufficient for the rider and other people working hard (e.g., the groom), less for spectators. This, of course, will vary with the weather. Pay careful attention to children: They are more susceptible to overheating than adults, since children's bodies don't produce as much sweat and therefore do not cool themselves as efficiently.

Transportation

Some larger barns bring golf carts or ATVs to shows so it is easier to get around the showgrounds, and some facilities offer golf carts for rent. A low-cost, easy-to-transport alternative is a decent mountain bike. A mountain

Getting around the showgrounds: If you have a golf cart, great, but old bikes do just as well.

bike is essential because most road bikes can't take the uneven dirt, mud, or grass terrain that is common at horse shows. However, a fancy mountain bike is not needed; it will only get beat up and will be more likely to be stolen. A cheap bike will do an adequate job of getting the biker from place to place.

LABELING

The Pony Club rally system is absolutely fanatical about labeling. And so it should be, since labeling cuts down on confusion and helps prevent equipment from getting lost. Any rally anywhere in the country has a huge flock of kids, some as young as seven or eight, with a copious amount of equipment that often looks the same, and no parents are allowed into the barn area to see that nothing gets lost or forgotten. A strength of the Pony Club rally is exactly that: no parents are allowed, so the kids learn to do for themselves and their horses and work together with their teammates, under the watchful eyes of the horse management judges who ensure that the kids and animals are safe (and on task!). Before a rally we always labeled all our equipment, and I mean *all* of it: everything from muck rakes to tack cleaning sponges to double-ended snaps!

In Pony Club we used our name, the name of our club, and the name of our region on our labels. Now that I have aged out of Pony Club, I usually just use my name. If you always travel to shows with the same group or barn, you can also put that name on your equipment. While someone

Labeling equipment (clockwise from top left): mailing labels, monogramming, Sharpie pen, permanent marker, 3-D fabric paint, brass halter plate.

finding a stray bucket may not know who Jane Doe is, she would be much more likely to know how to find Oakleaf Stables, especially if the bucket is labeled in Oakleaf's colors. The label should be easy to find, but for equipment you compete with, make sure it is also in an unobtrusive place so that it can't be seen while you're riding. For example, I write pertinent information in big block letters across the sides of my buckets, but for saddle pads I put labels on the spine of the pad under the gullet of my saddle.

LABELING EQUIPMENT

You won't be able to label everything the same way, so here are some ideas for what to use where:

Permanent Markers (Including Sharpies and Laundry Markers)

These work well for plastic items such as buckets, some fabrics, and even things like sponges. If you write METAL and BOOT POLISH in permanent ink across your rags, you will usually keep them straight. These markers are found in office supply stores and often supermarkets and drugstores as well. Despite the name, you will have to re-label things periodically as the ink will fade with use.

"Puffy" Paint (Three-Dimensional Fabric Paint)

This kind of paint comes in a small plastic bottle, and when you squeeze it, it comes out through the tip and dries in a raised line. You can buy it in craft stores in the fabric-craft section, and it is probably the best and most durable way you can label fabric and neoprene items such as bandages, wraps, galloping boots, saddle pads, and blankets. Best of all, you can label even dark-colored items by simply using white paint.

Monogramming

Although some people may see it as snobbery, I think embroidered monogramming is one of the most effective ways of identifying my equipment as my own. Years ago I chose one style of monogram that I put on anything I monogram: tack trunk cover, blankets, saddle covers, garment bags, boot bags, whatever. Monogramming is especially good for within-barn items, since often within a given barn everyone has the same colors. If your hunter-green-and-maroon saddle pad is the only one monogrammed, it will be pretty hard to lose in the shuffle. Anything you take out of the barn, however, should have your full name on it somewhere.

Stamping

My saddles have the innermost flap stamped with my name and driver's license number. The permanent identification may serve as a theft deterrent in itself, and even if taken I have a much better chance of recovering them. Your shoe repair or tack person will be able to do this for you.

Brass or Chrome Plates and Tags

I have saddle plates with my name on them on my saddles. These do nothing in the event of theft since they are easily removed, but they do provide easy identification around the barn. A halter plate is helpful both if the halter gets lost on its own and also if the horse should escape wearing it. My horses always wear halters with nameplates when away from home. I also have a small round bridle tag with my horse's name on his schooling bridle (I prefer for show bridles to remain uncluttered), and I have similar tags on his lead rope and stud chain. An item like a stud chain is remarkably easy to lose, which is such an annoyance because when you need one, you really need one. Labeling it will keep it from wandering too far off. You can order tags and plates through most tack stores and many mail order catalogs in a variety of fonts, sizes, and styles.

Stenciling

My Pony Club made stencils of the club's initials, PRPC, and spray-painted things with the stencil to label them. Stencilling is much more durable than permanent markers. Although we even did smaller items like sponges, it is probably most effective on large things like plastic tack trunks and muck buckets.

Mailing Labels

You can buy mailing labels fairly inexpensively through places such as Current (or other companies that sell checks), or through office supply or stationery stores. Get ones with a shiny (clear or metallic) surface, as they will wear better and be a little more water resistant than the sort with a papery surface. The advantage of mailing labels is that you can fit a good deal of information on them: name, phone number, barn or club name, address, horse's name, your zodiac sign, whatever. They work best for labeling items with a hard, smooth surface: grooming equipment, for example. You will increase the labels' lifespan if you cover them with strapping tape, which provides an extra layer of protection and some degree of waterproofing.

Colored Electrical Tape

Although you should have your name written somewhere on everything, electrical tape will tell you and others at a glance who something belongs to. In addition, if you label things in your "colors," you will add to the snappiness of your setup. I wind red electrical tape diagonally around the stick part of my muck rake, broom, and shovel (it looks like a barber pole or a candy cane when it's done), and then I can always pick mine out a mile away. Very small items that may be impractical to label otherwise, such as screw eyes, double snaps, or carabiners, can have a bit of tape wrapped around their middle to identify them as yours. No, it's not the end of the world if you lend a screw eye to your neighbor and you don't get it back—they cost all of seventy-nine cents or so—but it really can be an annoyance if you get to the next show and can't hang up your buckets or put up your stall guard because you're short a little piece of hardware. And even if your whole barn does their equipment in electrical tape the same way, it's likely that someone will see a taped stray tool or piece of equipment at a show when packing up to go home and take it back to the barn, knowing it probably belongs to someone from their barn. Once the item is home, it will be easier to sort out who its rightful owner is than it would be in the confusion of the showgrounds.

THE TRAVELING HORSE

THE TRAILER

First and foremost, make sure your truck and trailer are safe and well maintained. You are carrying very precious cargo, after all! Take your trailer to a reputable trailer repair shop once a year to have everything checked over and fixed. Pony Club puts out an excellent trailering manual which details what to do when in terms of trailer maintenance.

Most trailer maintenance will be done professionally, but cleaning you can do yourself. Wash the trailer with products made for car washing. You will need a telescoping or very long handled brush to reach up high on the walls and the ceiling. Use Armorall Tuff Stuff to get your tires looking spiffy, and Simple Green to clean away the grime in the crevices of your wheels. Once the trailer is dry, you can spray the exterior with kerosene (not near an open flame, of course), which will help it stay much cleaner on the trip.

Keep your truck and trailer well maintained and check them before each trip.

Before each trip, check the tire pressure in all your truck and trailer tires, the fluid levels (oil, fuel, coolant, transmission, windshield wiper, etc.) of your vehicle, and the turn signals and brake function. Do a walk-through in the trailer—a wasp's nest in a far corner would be a nightmare for your horse. Double check all your connections from the truck to the trailer: the hitch, safety chains, electrical, emergency brake, etc. These things only take a moment and are imperative for safe travel. Although a typical AAA plan will not help you if you break down with a truck and trailer, USRider's Equestrian Motor Plan will. They'll even help you find overnight accommodations for you and your stranded horse, and a vet if you need one. Their website is www.usrider.org, and their phone is 1-800-844-1409.

Ventilation is of prime importance while trailering. Always have at least some windows and vents open, even in very cold weather. Blanket heavily if you must, but horses need fresh air. If you are trailering more than one horse, ventilation is even more vital. Urine from even one horse can make the air quality unhealthy and unpleasant, but ventilation will allow the ammonia to dissipate. Horses create a lot of body heat, so having several horses in a small space will make that space very warm. Take this into account when blanketing, and open the windows.

BEDDING

People have mixed views on whether or not to put shavings, straw, or other bedding materials in the trailer. I always bed with something, not only for my horse but also to protect my floor boards. Urine and manure are strong substances that will eat away at your rubber mats and floor boards if left alone. Bedding the trailer soaks up urine and protects somewhat from manure. It also helps absorb odors, making the trip more comfortable for your horses. Shavings are less slippery but more dusty than straw, so unless you are transporting a horse with respiratory problems or a mare and foal, use shavings if you plan to bed your trailer.

PROTECTION

When he's in the trailer, your horse should wear some sort of protection against any bumps, bangs, strains, or scratches he might sustain as a result of his trip, not to mention kicks under the divider by an unfriendly neighbor. However, if you ship him commercially over a long distance, he almost certainly won't wear anything special, since the shippers do not want the liability of dealing with boots or bandages which may slip or shift or come undone during transit. And you probably wouldn't want someone you don't know bandaging your horse anyway. When you're doing the hauling yourself or you're going along with a friend, you can make sure that the protective equipment is fitted and stays fitted to your liking.

What protective equipment is needed? It depends on your horse and the length of your haul. If I'm hauling a quiet traveler twenty minutes or less, say to a lesson, I might just put on the brushing boots and bell boots that I'm going to ride in when I get there. For longer distances, I'll often use standing wraps and bell boots. Although I do shipping wraps sometimes, I find standing wraps and bell boots more secure, plus it's easier to get the tension consistent. I prefer wraps over shipping boots because wraps offer support to the tendons and ligaments in addition to protection against bangs and scrapes, while shipping boots only protect. Additionally, shipping boots are more likely to come off in the trailer. However, wraps will not protect the knees or hocks, and are easier to apply incorrectly than shipping boots. A

Dressed for travel: tail guard, shipping boots, fleece-covered halter.

good set of shipping boots (e.g., Lende International, Woof, or Dover Pro) will completely cover the knees and hocks, in addition to having a scuff plate at the heel. If you have a very difficult traveler, you can use shipping boots over standing wraps, but this arrangement is uncomfortable in warm weather.

If the haul will be long, I'll cover my horse's halter with sheepskin so that he won't get rubbed. Always ship in a leather halter so that, in an emergency, the halter will break instead of your horse. If your horse has very high head carriage with respect to the height of the ceiling or tends to toss his head, you can use a head bumper. Held in place by the halter's crownpiece, a head bumper fits over the horse's poll and will absorb some of the impact should the horse bang his head. Many horses will benefit from wearing a tail guard, which will protect the tail and keep it cleaner. In the trailer, the tail is the part of the spinal cord most vulnerable to bumps. A little added protection won't hurt. You can also put a polo wrap around the tail to provide protection.

Tie your horse in the trailer with something that either has breakaway capabilities or good stretching properties so that he won't get hurt if he pulls back. Most horses are fine with one tie, but some horses need two. I cross-tie Donovan because he has a penchant for trying to turn around in the trailer. If you tie a loop of rope baling twine (not plastic baling twine) to the trailer before attaching the trailer tie, it will break in an emergency. I also use a baling twine loop when tying to the outside of the trailer. Not only is it safer, but it's easier as well: it isn't always easy to get a lead rope tied properly in the small metal loops bolted onto the trailer.

FOOD AND WATER

I often haul horses with a little hay in front of them to keep them entertained. A horse with respiratory problems, however, should not have hay on the trailer. Do not feed a horse grain while he's trailering. Trailering is physically strenuous for the horse since he continually has to shift his weight to keep his balance. Some event riders will substitute a three- to four-hour haul for a gallop in their conditioning program. So feeding him grain while hauling would be like feeding him grain while riding: an invitation for colic. I offer water at each stop, usually every few hours. Most gas stations have water spigots if you haven't brought water from home. For more tips on water, see the discussion later on. Feed the horse carrots on the road; carrots provide a good source of hydration for a horse that is reluctant to drink. I usually don't unload the horse till the end of the day, because I find that it can be more stressful than beneficial for most horses to keep getting on and off the trailer in strange places. But I do take the horse for a long walk—at least forty-five minutes to an hour or so—upon arrival if I've been hauling all day.

STALL AND BARN SETUP

Once you have competed locally for a while and are comfortable with the rhythm and demands of competing, you may decide to undertake a longer trip to a multi-day show where you will need to stable your horse. This adds another dimension of complication but need not be unduly stressful if you have prepared appropriately. Most multi-day competitions have sufficient stabling on grounds, although some offer only offsite stabling or none at all (you should take this into account when deciding which shows

to attend). Your stabling is your barn away from home, but it will most likely come with few amenities, so be prepared to bring along everything you will need to take care of your horse and get him into the show ring as effortlessly as possible.

STORAGE

Often there is enough room in the barn aisle for you to put up a saddle rack, a bridle rack, and a blanket rack plus a folding chair or two and call it home. However, this is not always the case; some aisles are so narrow that even a few items would cause a safety hazard for horses and people passing through, and some shed-row style barns have little or no overhang so everything would get wet in the event of a cloudburst. Still, if I am traveling by myself, I generally try to have a couple important items in the aisle and work out of the trailer for the rest of my needs. Most of my things are in their own bags, which keeps them dust-free whether they're in the show barn or my trailer. The purchase of garment, helmet, boot, and bridle bags was one of the most practical investments I've ever made in terms of horse equipment. And I had them all monogrammed, which means that they are always easy to find among other people's similarly colored things.

If your trailer was stuffed to the gills just to transport your equipment to the showgrounds with overflow in the truck, it probably will not be practical for you to work out of it. However, if you have a walk-in dressing room like I do or even an ample tack compartment, you may find working out of your trailer convenient and economical. To keep your equipment safer, use a combination lock on your tack compartment or dressing room if possible; if not, you can buy a realtors' lock box from a locksmith shop and put a key in that. More secure than a Hide-A-Key, a realtors' lock box bolts or padlocks on to your trailer. It unlocks with a combination and holds your key inside, which means that you can lock your truck and trailer while you're riding without having to take your keys with you. Find out beforehand whether the trailer parking will be accessible from

Realtor lock boxes can keep your keys safe while you ride.

the barn or not. If it is close by and you have enough storage room in your trailer (e.g., a tack compartment or dressing room), you may be able to use that as your home base and just bring things to your stall as you need them. If the trailer parking is going to be some distance away, decide whether you'd rather drive things back and forth each day or cough up the extra money for a tack stall.

Although they are not always available due to space limitations, many shows allow you to reserve extra stalls for tack, feed, or grooming. If you are traveling with a group and split the cost, it won't set you back much to share a tack stall, and it may be more convenient because you won't have to move things back and forth each day. Bring a bicycle cable lock so that you can leave your things in the tack stall overnight.

I rarely use a tack stall because I usually find my trailer convenient, and I've used a feed stall even less frequently and a grooming stall not at all. A feed stall is only practical if you have an exceedingly large number of horses or you will be at the show for an exceedingly long time, say five days or more. Otherwise, I just run back and forth from my trailer a few times a day with hay and grain, which isn't bad even if it's far away. I will usually groom in my stall or tie to my trailer, but the advantage of having a grooming stall is that the horses' feet and legs will stay shavings-free, you can keep them from eating, and you can cross tie them while you work.

If you have a number of horses in your barn that usually share communal grooming equipment (which I discourage due to the likelihood of spreading skin problems and other diseases), it may be convenient to have the grooming equipment in one place and just bring the horses in by turn, instead of having to wander around the barn with a brushbox in tow. In your grooming stall, hang milk crates or small laundry baskets from the sides of the walls to keep your brushes, bottles, boots, and wraps handy. You can also arrange this setup in your tack stall. Grooming stalls are really only practical with large groups, but even then they can cause difficulties because it is inevitable that there will be multiple horses that need to get ready at once. The bottom line: If you're going by yourself, get a stall for your horse and a tack room if you really feel compelled to. If you're going in a small group, reserve a stall for your horse and a tack stall. If you're going in a big group, you can think about adding some extras if you feel so inclined, but you probably won't absolutely need them.

ESSENTIAL EQUIPMENT

Okay, we've discussed some optionals. Now let's get down to the essentials. (These are also listed in more succinct form in the packing list section later on.) For each horse you bring, you will need:

Two five-gallon water buckets with two double snaps or carabiners each (to allow for breakage, loss, or lending). Some people use big plastic garbage cans at shows, but they are more difficult to keep clean and full of fresh water because they are so big and unwieldy (try dragging a fifty-gallon trash can full of water out to dump because your horse has just pooped in it). Some horses will knock them over too, even if they're tied up, so they are not particularly safe. Steel used to climb in them (both front legs, water up to his elbows) and splash around until he got them to flip over and make a big flooded mess. I definitely recommend five-gallon water buckets!

One feed bucket or tub (include snaps or carabiners for buckets that can be hung).

Screw eyes. One for each bucket, one for each point of attachment for your stall guard (usually two or six, depending on the style of stall guard you have), plus several extras. String your screw eye collection on a piece of baling twine for ease of transportation and storage. If you wrap a bit of electrical tape around the raw ends of the baling twine, it becomes like a shoelace and you can tie and untie the twine without it unraveling.

One to two lengths baling twine. In some barns—metal ones, for example—you won't be able to put in screw eyes to hang your buckets and stall guards. In those cases, you can usually loop baling twine around the stall bars or something and tie it in a surgeon's knot, providing a sturdy place from which to hang your buckets. Some people use cable ties, but these are apt to loosen and break, so I avoid them.

Stall guard* if doors are not provided (this information should be in the prize list).

*A caveat about stall guards: Not all horses will respect all types of them. Donovan would simply walk through the big, solid vinyl ones, sending broken snaps and screw eyes flying. Steel would stay put with a single cable stall guard. No matter what, I advise against the grid-like nylon web stall guards: A horse could easily put a foot through them and injure himself. For Donovan I have also used a portable stall screen, more of a gate or grate really, which allows him to stick his head out and visit with passersby but doesn't give him the option of bursting out; it is hung so that it opens inward, which means that if he leans on it, he would have to take down the whole door frame to get out.

Bridle rack. If accessible to the horse it should be taken down whenever he is unsupervised—it would be easy for a horse to snag a lip or gouge an eye on one, but it is very convenient to have extra hooks by your stall!

Folding saddle rack. Whether this is in the aisle or in the tack room, you need at least one per horse. If you've got multiple saddles as at an event, you might consider two. I like the folding kind best because they're easy to transport and store, and the little rack underneath the saddle part is great for storing boots or bandages. There are also stacked saddle racks so that you can hang multiple saddles on the wall and have more floor space.

Two to three bales of shavings or two bales of straw for initial bedding, plus one more bale of shavings every other day or so, or one-half additional bale of straw every day (amounts to be added approximate). Find out beforehand whether bedding will be available for purchase at the show. If it will, buying it there may be easier and occasionally more economical than bringing it, depending on how cheaply you can get it at home and how expensive gas is.

Grain and hay from home. If you will be away from home for several weeks, it may be impossible to bring feed for the whole trip, but bring as much as you can and introduce the new feed gradually in combination with the feed to which your horse is accustomed. If you're going to be gone several days or are bringing hay for several horses from the same barn, you can bring it in intact bales. If you're only going to be gone a night or two and won't need much, put individual feedings in plastic garbage bags. If you tie the bags shut, be sure to poke holes in them so that the hay can breathe—if it gets warm, hay may get hot and combust or get moldy. Be particularly careful with legume hay such as alfalfa which has a high moisture content to begin with. The nice thing about premeasuring like this is that you don't have to do it at the show, plus bagged hay is less messy than an open bale.

Pack your grain in brown paper grocery bags, double bagging for big rations. Many people use Ziploc plastic bags, but grain will easily ferment or mold in these, especially in show season heat. Put your grain in the bottom of the bag and fold the bag over itself in thirds where the creases are, just as it would be folded if it didn't have anything in it and you wanted to store it. Wind strapping tape around the bundle and it should stay securely closed. (Duct tape, much to my disillusionment, does not work well on paper bags. Too bad—I thought duct tape could do anything!) With a permanent marker, clearly label each bag of grain or hay (use duct tape or wide masking tape to create a writing surface on the garbage bag) with the horse's name, the contents of the bag, and which feeding it is: Amelia, Thursday p.m., two pounds oats. That way, if something should happen to you, others will be able to determine when your horse was last fed, and also what your horse's regular food is if he should be under different care beyond the show.

Box fan secured with bungee cords.

Box fan (if the weather is hot and you have access to electricity). You can secure it with baling twine, but make sure you have an ample extension cord and a splitter if you're far from the outlet.

Blanket rack (if the weather is such that you will need a blanket, sheet, cooler, sweat sheet, or fly sheet). Instead of a conventional blanket rack, I usually just use a single cable stall guard with double snaps at the end, snapped onto my stall door via a couple loops of baling twine.

Stall card. This is something I grew up with in Pony Club that I'd like to see more competitors at recognized shows utilize. It is preventative medicine, really. Include the following:

• *Horse's name and your name and phone number.* At the very least, put your horse's name on the stall, along with your name and the phone number where you can be reached. I always list my cell phone, but if you put your hotel phone number, be sure to note in whose name the hotel room is reserved so you can be found.

• *Your horse's age, sex, breed, and color.* A picture helps too, in the event that he gets lost (unlikely, but it does happen!). Leaving a halter on your horse at all times when on the showgrounds (leather, please, so that it will break in the event that he gets stuck on something) will make it easier to catch him should he go for a midnight stroll. And having a nameplate on his halter helps even more—his finder will know who he is and will more easily be able to return him to his temporary digs.

- *Your horse's resting vital signs (TPR): temperature, pulse, and respiration, any known allergies, insurance info, plus the name and phone numbers of his home vet and farrier.* If your horse is ill, there is a readily available baseline of what your horse is like when he's well.
- *Your horse's food, including time and amounts.* If something should happen to you, others will know what to feed him.
- *Any vices.* If your horse is prone to kick, bite, or whatever, that is a useful warning for someone who goes in to help him if he is colicking or gets cast or otherwise is in trouble.

OTHER NECESSARY ITEMS

(These can be shared by several people if you're traveling with a group)

Wheelbarrow or muck bucket and cart. Although wheelbarrows are big and are a nightmare to transport because they take up so much room, they will make your life easier once you're at the show; instead of having to make multiple trips to the muck pile when cleaning a stall, you can do it in one with a moderately-sized wheelbarrow. And they are invaluable if you have to strip a stall. Transport your wheelbarrow in your dressing room, empty horse slot in the trailer, in the back of your pickup, or strapped to your roof rack. Bungee cords or baling twine will help keep it in place.

Manure fork. I like the plastic-tined "Future Fork" style of muck rakes best. Their closely set tines make it easy to pick out wet spots and separate clean shavings from balls of manure. With use, you will probably have to re-tighten the bolt that holds the fork part on the handle part.

Rake. This will help you keep your aisle tidy.

Pitchfork, shovel, broom, and rake for stall and aisle maintenance.

Broom. For asphalt or concrete aisles, sweep after feeding and mucking to keep things looking nice. Even if you're not much of a neatnik, you should still have a broom to clean the shavings out of the hinge on your trailer ramp. I like pushbrooms best if I've got a big aisle to do, but a normal straw broom is more versatile.

Large plastic shovel. This will come in handy when you're stripping your stall or loading shavings into your stall or trailer.

Cordless drill. Although there will usually be holes reasonably located holes for your screw eyes, this will not always be the case, so you should be prepared. I recommend a cordless drill because in temporary barns you probably won't have an electrical outlet; even if you do, it may not be close enough to your stall. Be sure the drill is fully charged before you leave home, unless you have an electrical outlet in your trailer.

Flashlight and fire extinguisher. Keep these close at hand (e.g., just inside the tackroom door or near your horse's stall) so they're readily available if needed.

Basic tool kit. Include a hammer, two screwdrivers (Phillips and flathead), leather punch, pocket knife, scissors, adjustable crescent wrench, pliers, measuring tape, and assorted nails and screws. The most important items will be the hammer and pliers for pulling out random bits of metal (such as staples), safety hazards that are sure to be stuck in your horse's stall. You will use the screwdrivers for setting up your screw eyes: Insert the screwdriver into the screw eye, almost up to the handle for leverage, and twist.

Stepping stool. This will come in handy both for braiding and for mounting, and also will function as an extra chair.

Chairs (folding, camping, director's, etc.). Bring something easy to transport that will give you a place to take a load off. There always seem to be lots of family and friends spectating and supporting at shows and they will be happy to have a place to sit down, too.

Bulletin board w/ pushpins or thumbtacks. Not absolutely necessary, but handy to have to keep important pieces of paper or schedules within reach. Only use one if you're setting up a tack stall; this is *not* a piece of equipment to keep in the aisle.

Hand soap. Most Port-a-Potties don't have soap in them, and during the course of the day you'll use the Port-a-Potty, muck out your stall, polish boots, and probably eat with your hands. Yuck! Bring some hand soap to rid yourself of at least a few layers of germs and grime!

Hose or empty two-and-a-half gallon corn oil jug. Hoses are a tremendous asset at competitions. Not only can you bathe your horse, but you can haul water without busting your back and without sloshing half of it into your shoes by the time you get from the spigot to your stall. You don't even need a nozzle on the end: Fold the hose one to three times, depending on the water pressure, and you can keep the water from spraying until you've reached your bucket. A hose on a reel or a self-coiling hose are the easiest to store neatly. Hoses do take up a lot of space and can be somewhat of a liability (they will undoubtedly be borrowed and possibly broken by other competitors unless you take them away after every use, which is even more of a pain), so if you'd prefer not to deal with them you can prevent the sore back/wet sock syndrome by washing out a large corn oil jug and using it for water. Since it has a cap you can screw on, no water sloshes out, and since it is only half the volume of a water bucket, it's easier to carry. I especially like the convenience of filling the corn oil jug before I leave the barn in the evening; that way, if I come back later that night to check on the horses and top off the water, I don't have to spend my time bumbling around in the dark. Or if I arrive at the barn early in the morning and I'm in a hurry, I can easily refill my horse's water without it taking any time at all.

First aid kits, human and equine. In the packing lists given later, I have a list of all the materials I take in my first aid kits, which is essentially the same as what is required at Pony Club rallies. You may want to take a few extra items, depending on your own personal needs and your horse's. For example, Donovan kept breaking out in hives one July, so I took a packet of Azium wherever I went. It is not legal to compete under Azium, so if I used it I would need to scratch, but my vet and I decided it should be handy in case the horse had another attack and needed immediate medication.

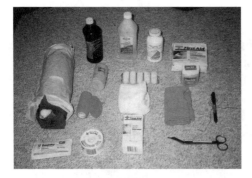

An equine first aid kit may include hydrogen peroxide, rubbing alcohol, phenylbutazone, sterile gauze pads, ace bandages, Naquasone, Vaseline, Vetrap, clean rag, thermometer, Banamine, waterproof tape, rolled gauze, bandage scissors.

HOME AWAY FROM HOME

Some horses settle into their show stabling settings better than others. If your horse seems anxious or worried, don't be too concerned. If he is young or hasn't been away from home much, he will probably soon become more laid back about unfamiliar surroundings. Donovan's first show was also his first time away from home, and the day we arrived I thought he was going to have a nervous breakdown or colic at the very least. He could not stand still for the life of him; he paced circles in his stall and whinnied. He wouldn't even eat—very uncharacteristic for this horse. The only time he seemed at all calm was when I was right there in the stall with him. I thought I might have to camp out with him for the night! Thankfully, when I came back later that evening to check on him, he seemed to have settled in a bit. The next day was even better, and by the last day he was completely comfortable with his surroundings and seemed to enjoy the adventure of being away from home. At his second show, he got off the trailer and looked around anxiously for about a minute before apparently realizing, "Oh, this is just another show," and calming down. By the third show he was completely unconcerned and even enthusiastic and curious about being in a new and different place.

Always handwalk your horse frequently at shows. This will help settle a worried or inexperienced horse since it accustoms him to the surroundings in a nonthreatening way. He will experience all the sights and sounds of the show without having to focus on his work at the same time, which is also a comfort to you, the rider, because you know that most things won't be completely foreign to him as you are doing your medium trot across the diagonal or trying to get him down the line to the next oxer. Handwalking is important even for the most laid-back horse; frequently, stalls at horse shows are smaller than the stall your horse has at home, so it is good for his joints and muscles to stretch periodically in an environment where there is no turnout.

I advise always using a stud chain when walking a horse in unfamiliar surroundings, particularly for a young horse, no matter how quietly he usually leads. Donovan was very well-mannered to lead at home (I could probably lead him by his forelock if I needed to!), but sometimes shows can be very exciting and when he was young he needed a little extra reminder that leaping through the air wasn't okay! Anytime he went out of his stall he had a stud chain on. I might have used it once or even not at all at any given show, but for that one time I needed it, I was glad it was there! Make sure also that you have a cotton lead rope (the thicker ones are better) since they are easier to hang on to and won't burn your hands as badly as the nylon ones should your horse pull away from you. If you're walking a particularly frisky horse, wear gloves to give you more protection and traction, and use a cotton longe line instead of a lead rope so that if your horse tries to get away, you will be much more likely to still be hanging on to the end of him!

IN THE STALL

Water

Even when Donovan was very concerned on the first day at his first show, he still drank water. Not all horses will do this: many will not drink water that tastes different from what they are used to at home, and as you know from the rider-hydration discussions, water is absolutely essential for any athlete!

If the show is a one-day affair, consider taking water from home. You can have a water tank of various sizes installed in your trailer. Another option is to use the big five-gallon water cooler jugs from bottled water delivery services. You are not likely to find a company that will sell them to you, but if you use their service once a month or so you will usually find yourself with some empty bottles on hand before they are replaced. Just remember to save the big plastic bottle caps when you open the water so that you have a way to keep your horse's water from spilling. If your horse uses supplements that come in large lidded buckets (e.g. Strongid C, Farrier's Formula), those buckets, once empty, are useful for bringing water from home too. You can also get big water containers from camping stores.

Even if your horse is good about drinking strange water, bringing it from home still may be a better solution for a one-day show. When there is no stabling, the water source may be quite a ways from where you are parked. Bringing water will save you from having to go hunt it down and lug it across the showgrounds, spilling half of it on the way!

If bringing water from home is unfeasible for whatever reason, try flavoring your horse's water with a little apple juice at home a week or two before the show. Then at the show, put apple juice in the strange water. The horse will taste the familiar flavor of apple juice which will mask the unfamiliar flavor of the water. Some people use other flavorings such as Kool-Aid or Jello, but I prefer a natural flavoring to an artificial one that has artificial colors as well. Moreover, not all horses will accept Kool Aid flavors, but most horses like apple juice—it has a natural taste that they recognize from eating apples. Many horses also like Gatorade, which has the added benefit of providing electrolytes, although it also has artificial colors and flavors. You can use a little of the powdered Gatorade or a splash of the liquid kind.

If your horse likes to dunk his food in the water, take a small, aquarium-sized fishnet with you so that you can skim out the hay and grain without having to dump the whole bucket of water each time. At home, a catfish in a large water trough is enough to keep the water supply clean from algae, but as catfish aren't practical for the road, you should simply scrub your water buckets with dish detergent, bleach (be sure to let the buckets air out for a day or so so that the excess chlorine will evaporate), or apple cider vinegar.

Bedding

Because of disposal or supplier arrangements, some shows will allow only straw or only shavings for bedding. If your horse is accustomed to bedding on straw and he will be on shavings at the show, there shouldn't be much of a problem unless he is very sensitive. Some horses have respiratory difficulties from the dust if they are on shavings; dampening the shavings with water in a spray bottle will help. Other horses will break out in hives due to allergies to certain types of shavings; if this happens, call the vet (he will probably give the horse an antihistamine). Note the type of shavings the horse reacted to and bed on a different type the next time. Do not ever bed on black walnut shavings—they are toxic to horses.

If you usually bed on shavings and the show allows only straw, your horse may decide that munching on straw around the clock is a great way to entertain himself. This form of diversion is not harmless, however; it may cause him to colic. If he looks like he's going to eat his bedding, put PineSol (or Eqyss McNasty Anti-Chewing Spray) in a spray bottle and spray down the bedding, making sure to avoid his hay. He won't want to eat it anymore!

STUDS

Depending on the ground, you may want to put studs in your horse's shoes for dressage, cross-country, show jumping, or hunters. Which studs you choose will depend on whether the

An assortment of studs.

ground is soft, slippery, hard, deep, whatever. Talk to your instructor or a knowledgeable friend about which ones are appropriate for the weather and footing you will encounter that day. Malcolm Kelley has written a good book on studs called, appropriately enough, *The Stud Book,* which will give you an idea of what studs you need to have in your collection.

Make sure your horse is drilled and tapped (that is, that his shoes have the appropriate threaded holes so that you can screw in the studs) before you leave home. There are various kinds of materials you can put in the holes when there are no studs in them, but I find oiled cotton plugs to be the easiest

Stud kit essentials (left to right): Top row: WD-40, Stud Suds (for cleaning studs), cotton plugs; Bottom row: Tee tap, wire prep brush, horse shoe nail, adjustable crescent wrench.

to use. Clean out the stud holes with a small wire brush (shaped like a bristly pipe cleaner), and twist the cotton plugs in firmly. To dig foreign material out of the stud holes, use a horseshoe nail.

Spray the stud hole and stud with WD-40 to facilitate insertion of the stud. Use a small, adjustable crescent wrench to tighten the stud in place. I find it easiest to work on studs if I'm seated on a sturdy step stool and have the horse's foot placed on a towel in my lap. Once you take the studs out, rinse all the mud and grime off with water, then coat them in corn oil to prevent them from rusting. Alternatively, there are special soaking solutions (e.g., Stud Suds) made specifically for cleaning studs; you can find them at Dover and at eventing-oriented tack stores such as Bit of Britain.

COUNTDOWN!

Make sure you arrive at the showgrounds with plenty of time to do everything you need to do before you ride. If you're at an event or dressage show, you know exactly what time you need to be ready. If you're at a hunter/jumper show, you can guesstimate it fairly accurately based on the times posted for each class or set of classes to start, and on the number of competitors in each class. Begin with your ride time and count down backwards, allotting an appropriate amount of time for each thing you have to do before you go in the ring. Say you have your first ride of the day at 10:14. How much time do you need to warm up? It depends on you and your horse and other factors such as weather, but let's say forty-five minutes, which puts you at 9:29. You're shooting to be on your horse at 9:29. Now allow yourself one hour to get ready—start at 8:29. Yes, I know that's a lot of time, and I know that at home you can get ready in a tenth of the time. But you're at a show, so your equipment isn't in the same place it usually is, your horse needs to be cleaner than he usually is, and you're wearing more clothes than you usually do. Allowing yourself an hour will give you time to

Jennifer and Steel ready to go cross country. Photo by Deborah Ravinsky.

find and assemble all your grooming equipment and tack, fix that unraveling braid, find your number if you've lost it, or deal with whatever mini-crisis you might encounter.

What do you need to have finished before you start getting ready? If it's an overnight show, feeding, watering, and stall cleaning. If you are with a group, all the horses should be fed at the same time so they don't get worried. Whoever has the earliest ride time (and therefore arrives first) will usually get the privilege of feeding the whole barn. If you're there on your own, perhaps you can trade off morning feeding duties with your neighbors. Also factor in the time it takes to arrive at the show from your lodgings. On your way to the motel the first night, time how long it takes to get there so you'll know for the morning, but remember to allow for the possibility of rush hour traffic if you're showing during the week, or holiday traffic if it's a holiday weekend. Websites such as maps.google.com or www.mapquest.com give estimated driving times that are often quite accurate. If it's a one-day show that you're hauling into from home, figure out how long it will take you to get from your house to your barn, get hitched up, get your horse dressed to go and then on the trailer, and then the actual drive time as well. Then allow time for getting your number (there may be a long line at the secretary's office) and finding a parking place, etc. It will always be easier if it's a show you've been to before and you know how the facility is laid out. Once you've decided how long you need from the time you leave your house or motel until the time you need to start getting ready, you will know what time you need to get up. I will often build in an extra hour or half-hour, depending on the distance I need to travel and my familiarity with the competition. It is helpful to write all this down so you know exactly what you need to be doing when, so that you will end up ready to go at the appropriate time. For example:

9:14	Ride
8:29	Warmup
7:29	Get ready
6:45	Feed, water, hay, and muck
6:20	Leave motel
5:50	Wake up

AT THE LAST MINUTE

If you're lucky enough to have someone there to help you before you go into the ring, have him or her bring a bucket containing at least fly spray, rags for wiping your horse and your boots, a brush, and water for you and your horse. Spare tack parts, such as stirrup leathers, reins, or girths, never hurt either. If you've warmed up with boots or bandages on your horse, your helper can take them off for you. If you've warmed up with a whip but you're not allowed to compete with one, leave the whip with the helper. If it's windy and your horse suffers from static cling, have him

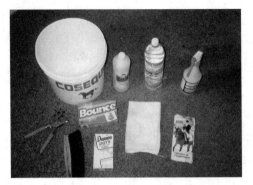

"Last minute bucket," including (clockwise from top left) rubbing alcohol, water, fly spray, dressage tests (for dressage or eventing), rub rag, sugar cubes, brush, leather hole punch, Bounce anti-static sheets.

wiped down with a Bounce anti-static fabric sheet to reduce the static.

If it's hot, your helper can hold your coat while you're warming up and can sponge your horse down before you go in, using a mixture of one bottle of rubbing alcohol and one to two gallons of water. Because of the evaporation from the alcohol, your horse will feel much cooler and perkier going into the ring. If you're going into the dressage ring, you will want your horse to have nice white foam around his mouth, but if you're going into the hunter ring you won't. Depending on what's appropriate, your helper can either wipe the foam off or encourage more by feeding your horse a couple of apple slices or sugar cubes. If you're competing in dressage, rinse any residual hay out of your horse's mouth with a big, needleless syringe before tacking up so that his foam isn't green. Take a swig of water, have your helper spritz a little fly spray on your horse, and you're ready to go!

ICE AND POULTICE TREATMENTS

After you've cooled your horse out and cleaned him up, consider the amount of work he did and on what kind of footing. If he worked really hard, he might benefit from being sponged down in a fifty-fifty solution of liniment and alcohol to soothe tired muscles. You can also put liniment on his legs, and on yourself if you're sore too! Available from health food stores, arnica is another good remedy for sore tissues; you can smear it on in cream or gel form, or take it orally in little white sugary pills, which dissolve well in water for horses. If I galloped on hard

ground, I like to ice my horse's legs and poultice them. The ice boots that extend from above the knee and hock to the ground are great because they can ice almost the whole leg. They can be difficult to use, however; it seems like there are millions of little pockets which fit only a few ice cubes each, and they take forever to fill! If you are icing only the lower legs, you can use bags of frozen peas or corn, which

Post-ride leg care (clockwise from top left): poultice, liniment, ice, frozen corn for icing.

mold well to the shape of the horse's leg. Hold them in place with brushing boots. Once they've melted, you can refreeze them to use for icing the next time.

Poulticing draws the heat and inflammation out of the horse's legs. Smear the poultice generously on the legs, and then cover with wet brown paper bags, wet paper, or wet sheet cotton. I like the sheet cotton option the best because it molds easily to the leg. Wrap with standing bandages as usual, and leave the poultice on overnight before rinsing it off in the morning.

LAUNDRY

Let's face it. Everything gets dusty, muddy, and/or dirty when it's around horses—clothes, equipment, people. Super-effective laundry skills are a must if you're a horse person.

It is best if you can wash show items the day after you return home if at all possible. The longer a stain sits, the more difficult it is to remove. Always be sure to read the labels of the item before washing it; although hotter water is better at getting things clean, it may melt, shrink, or otherwise damage some types of fabric. Bleach will whiten better than anything out there, but be sure that whatever you're bleaching is bleachable! All rules for "normal laundry" apply to horse laundry too: separate darks from whites, put detergent in the empty tub and add clothes once the tub is partially filled with water, use powdered detergent for more cleansing oomph (plus it's more economical), use Clorox 2, Oxi-Clean, or another color-safe bleach or bleach alternative to keep colors bright, etc. Once you've run your muddy, sandy, hairy horse equipment through the washer, use a damp paper towel to remove dirt and hair from the washer, then run a second empty cycle so that the next load of laundry won't end up dirtier than it was when it started. Here are a few more tips.

BLANKETS

Although I am a staunch supporter of the "do-it-yourself" mentality, blanket washing is one area in which it usually pays to have a professional do it. Especially if the blanket is washed only once per season, as they often are, a blanket washing service is more likely to get the blanket really clean than you are at home. If you'd rather wash your blanket yourself, take it to a laundromat (go at a time when you expect it to be fairly empty—most people will not take kindly to the idea of you stuffing a filthy, smelly horse blanket into one of the machines), and use a large, front-load washing machine only. Do not use the top-loading kind that you have at home—these are too small and completely ineffective for blanket washing. For a front-load washing machine you will only need to use half the amount of detergent as usual. If your blanket is waterproof, you may want to use a product made specifically for that type of treated fabric. Rambo makes a good waterproof blanket wash. If you'd rather use normal detergent, use powdered instead of liquid. Line dry (hang up) the blanket after washing.

SHEETS (HORSE, NOT BED!)

These you can wash at home in your normal top-load washer. Heavier sheets should be washed individually; lighter sheets such as fly sheets may be washed two at a time. If they are particularly dirty, pre-treat the filthiest parts with liquid detergent and allow it to sit for the amount of time recommended on the detergent label. You can also pre-soak by adding detergent to the tub, filling with water, and letting the sheet sit in the full tub of water for an hour or more. Then complete the wash cycle. Some sheets you can dry in the dryer, but others will melt or shrink. Read the label, but if in doubt always line dry.

SADDLE PADS

Colored saddle pads are easy: just throw them in the wash and line or machine dry (line drying will extend their life, but it's not always practical). White saddle pads, which you probably use if you do dressage, eventing (for the dressage phase, at least), or hunters, are a little more complicated. After use, they will probably be stained black or brown where they came in contact with the saddle and horse sweat, and they will probably have a little black from your boots as well. Scrub liquid detergent into the stains and allow to sit for about ten to fifteen minutes if possible. Using powdered detergent and bleach if possible (bleach alternative if not), wash at the hottest temperature that the fabric will tolerate. Once they are done in the washing machine, check the pads for any stains that remain, and re-pre-treat and wash again. This is important, because stubborn stains are more difficult to remove if the saddle pad is allowed to dry first. Since white pads are easier to keep looking nice if they are never allowed to get overly dirty, I recommend changing pads every ride, or if this is not practical, at least every day.

GALLOPING OR BRUSHING BOOTS

Velcro boots should be velcroed closed or to another boot to prevent tangling. Wash in warm or cold water with detergent, and allow to drip dry. You can also hand-wash your boots. If you must put them in the dryer, put them on air dry (no heat) because heat will hurt the neoprene. If you have leather boots, allow them to dry several hours after washing and rub conditioner into them while they're still slightly damp. As long as you condition them properly and use a mild detergent (e.g., Woolite) or a leather washing product (e.g., Pepede), there is no need to shy away from machine-washing leather galloping boots.

BANDAGES AND WRAPS

Velcro the bandages together and put them in an old pillowcase tied shut with a shoelace or an old sock. This will keep them from tangling. You can also use laundry bags specifically made for washing bandages. Machine wash warm, and line dry if possible or machine dry if the label says it is okay. No matter what, you will extend the life of your bandages if you line dry.

BRUSHES

To control the spread of skin afflictions or to keep from adding dirt to a clean horse, wash your brushes in the washing machine with detergent and warm water. To disinfect, add bleach. Most brushes tend to float to the top of the water; to counteract this effect place them in an old pillowcase tied shut with a shoelace or an old sock. This will also prevent them from scratching the washing machine.

BREECHES

Most riding clothes (except coats, which you must dry clean unless you have a washable one) you can wash as you would any other items of apparel, but breeches may require some special care. Some breeches must be dry cleaned. Breeches with faux leather, faux suede, or Clarino knee patches or full seats shouldn't be very complicated: just wash in warm or cool water and hang dry. Breeches with real suede or leather can be washed in a special leather care product such as Pepede, or you can use regular detergent or something mild like Woolite. If you spray the suede or the flesh side of the leather with Pam cooking spray before you wash them, they won't come out as stiff. Line dry. While the breeches are still damp, roll the leather in your hands to maintain its suppleness. After a number of washes the leather or suede will probably stiffen up to some extent. If the leather is really stiff, rub leather conditioner on the inside (the surface that comes in contact with your skin) and allow to soak in. This is easier if the leather is still a little damp. If it's not too stiff yet, you can use hand or body lotion instead, which will probably make your legs feel less greasy!

CROSS COUNTRY VESTS

Wash in cool water with detergent and drip dry, or as specified on the label. Since the foam in these vests makes them float, wash them with other heavier items (bath towels work well) and put the vests on the bottom.

FINAL WORDS

If you have been doing your homework with your riding and if you've read and understood this book, chances are excellent that you are ready to go to your next (or first!) competition. You're ready to ride, and you and your horse look the part. You both are appropriately turned out. Your stall, equipment, and trailer are safe and clean, and you are prepared for almost any occurrence. Congratulations! Now go and have fun.

A competition isn't just about competing. It's about setting a goal and working to achieve it, whether that goal be to qualify for a four-star, three-day event or post on the correct diagonal. It's about being with friends and watching and cheering them on in their rides and enjoying their goodwill when they support yours. It's about good fun sport in the outdoors. But more than anything, it's about your bond with your horse. This is a special undertaking between the two of you. So enjoy the time away from your normal commitments of job, family, school, and get to know your horse a little better. Hang out with him in his stall, take him for walks, pet him and give him love. Your already-solid partnership will only improve!

HELPFUL LISTS

I love lists. I write lists for everything: to do, grocery, goals, chores, packing...sometimes I even write a list of the lists I need to write! Here I've listed a few resources that you may find helpful.

COMPETITION CHECKLISTS

A CAVEAT EMPTOR

These 'to do' and packing lists given are samples of my checklists. I'm providing them here because they may help when you're formulating your own checklists. *Your* checklists will necessarily be different from *my* checklists because we have different horses, we live in different parts of the country, we're competing at different times of the year at different facilities, and we like to use different equipment. I don't believe it is possible to take a generic list out of a book, follow it precisely, and arrive at the show grounds with the appropriate collection of stuff.

I keep several different lists around and use the one appropriate for the length and type of competition I'm going to. I also keep extended and short versions of each list: the short version only includes things that don't live in the trailer (so I know what to pack from home and the barn), while the long version includes everything that I think I might need while I'm gone, including things that are always in the trailer. The extended version is most useful at the beginning of the season when I might need to replace or refill equipment or supplies that were worn out or used up during the prior season.

So I encourage you to look at these for inspiration, guidelines, structure, etc., and write your own, with any omissions or additions that are appropriate for your specific circumstances.

To Do: The Day Before Leaving

- ❑ Pack clothes
- ❑ Ride horse
- ❑ Bathe horse
- ❑ Clip horse
- ❑ Pack grain
- ❑ Load hay
- ❑ Clean tack
- ❑ Polish boots
- ❑ Memorize tests (for dressage shows or events)
- ❑ Check truck/trailer (brakes, lights, fluid levels, etc)
- ❑ Wash saddle pads, brushes, sheets, etc.
- ❑ Braid (if riding early the next morning)
- ❑ Load equipment

One-Day Dressage Packing List (Short)

Revised 2/18
For: Denville-Kanani Dressage
Date: Feb 21

I. Tack
   A. Schleese
      1. Dressage girth
      2. Supracor pad
   B. Passier bridle w/bit
II. Legs
   A. Standing wraps
   B. Flannel bandages
   C. Bell boots
III. Grooming
   A. Grooming kit
   B. Eye ointment/aloe heal
   C. Sugar cubes
   D. Fly spray
IV. Artificial aids
   A. HS spurs
V. Blankets
   A. Rain sheet
   B. Polarfleece cooler
VI. Barn equipment
   A. Haynet
   B. (Grain)
VII. Dressage Clothes
   A. White gloves
   B. Stock tie, pin
   C. Shirt
   D. Belt
   E. White full seat breeches
VIII. Other clothes
   A. T shirt

B. Sweatshirts
C. CNDC/winter jacket
D. Vest
E. Skort
F. Shorts
I. Extra underwear/socks
J. Barn clogs
K. Muck boots
L. Hat
M. Jeans
IX. Personal
   A. Sunscreen
   B. Sunglasses
   C. Water
   D. Backpack
      1. Tylenol
      2. Arnica
      3. Maps, directions
      4. Omnibus, Rulebook
      5. Tests
      6. Extra socks/underwear
      7. Video
   E. Cooler
      1. Fruit
      2. Food
      3. Ice
   F. Purse
      1. Wallet w/money
      2. Checkbooks
      3. Cell phone + charger

Overnight Event Packing List (Extended)

For: Waredaca

Date: June 3

I. Tack
  A. Schleese
    1. Dressage girth + extra
    2. Show pad
    3. Schooling pad
  B. Passier
    1. Girth + extra
    2. Poly pad
  C. Passier bridle w/bit
  D. Schooling bridle w/bit
  E. Figure 8 bridle w/bit
  F. Longeing equipment
    1. Longe line
    2. Side reins
    3. Longe whip
  G. Show halter
  H. Spare tack
    1. Dressage girth
    2. Jumping girth
    3. Halter
    4. Bridle
    5. Stirrup irons/leathers
    6. Lead rope
  I. Stud chain
  J. Fly mask
  K. Lead rope
II. Legs
  A. Standing wraps
  B. Flannel bandages
  C. Woof boots
  D. Bell boots x 2
  E. Extra shoes

  F. Shipping boots
III. Grooming
  A. Grooming kit
    1. Curry comb x 3
    2. Dandy brush
    3. Body brush x 2
    4. Rub rag (1/day)
    5. Hairbrush
    6. Hoof pick
    7. Hoof dressing
    8. Pledge
  B. Braiding kit
    1. Scissors
    2. Rubber bands
    3. Yarn
    4. Thread
    5. Pull through
    6. Needles
    7. Hair clips
    8. Fine toothed comb
    9. Pulling comb
    10. Small sponge
    11. Spray bottle
    12. Seam ripper
    13. Pen
    14. Stool
  C. Bathing stuff
    1. Shampoo
    2. Detangler
    3. Listerine
    4. Selsun Blue

5. 3 sponges
    a. Body
    b. Dock/sheath
    c. Face
6. Grooma Loopa mitt
7. Grooming mitt
8. Wash bucket
(9. Hose)
D. Liniment
E. Poultice
F. Paper bags
IV. Artificial aids
  A. Bat
  B. Schooling whip
  C. Spurs
V. Blankets
  A. Show sheet
  B. Polarfleece cooler
  C. Rain sheet
  D. Quarter sheet
  E. Fly sheet
  F. Rambo (if weather req)
VI. Barn equipment
  A. 2 water buckets w/snaps
  B. Water jug/hose
  C. Feeding
    1. Feed tub
    2. Salt
    3. Corn oil
    4. Grain (5 feedings)
    5. Hay (2 bales)
    6. Grain storage can
  D. Wheelbarrow
  E. Pitchfork
  F. Broom/rake
  G. Shovel

H. Stall guard
I. Box fan w/bungees
J. Extension cord
VII. Tack room equipment
  A. Tack cleaning kit
    1. Castile soap
    2. Water container
    3. Sm tack sponges
    4. Toothbrush
    5. Dental pick
    6. Dental floss
    7. Toothpaste
    8. Neverdull metal polish
    9. Clean rags
    10. Passier Lederbalsam
    11. Tack cleaning hook
  B. Boot cleaning kit
    1. Small tack sponges
    2. Castile soap
    3. Water container
    4. Rags
    5. Black leather dye
    6. Black wax shoe polish
    7. Neutral cream polish
    8. Toothbrush
    9. Shoe brush
    10. Black edge dressing
    11. Nylons
    12. Blitzglanz
  C. Tool kit
    1. Hammer
    2. Phillips screwdriver
    3. Flathead screwdriver
    4. Crescent wrench
    5. Pliers
    6. Tape measure

7. Nails

8. Screw eyes

9. Cordless drill

10. Leather punch

11. Scissors

12. Jack knife

13. Baling twine

D. Equine first aid kit

   1. Practical cotton

   2. 2" wide gauze

   3. 2 rolls Vetrap

   4. Thermometer & clip

   5. 4" sterile cotton pads

   6. Bandage scissors

   7. Alcohol

   8. 1" medical tape

   9. Aloe Heal/Furazone

   10. Betadine

   11. Petroleum jelly

   12. Latex gloves

E. Human first aid kit

   1. Band-Aids

   2. Tylenol

   3. Antibiotic cream

   4. Nail scissors

   5. Aloe

   6. Bug bite gel

F. Boot hooks

G. Boot jack

H. Saddle rack

I. Bridle rack

J. Blanket rack

K. Flashlight

L. Fire extinguisher

VIII. Dressage/Show Jumping Attire

A. Velvet helmet

B. White gloves

C. Black gloves

D. Shirts x 2

E. Stock tie x 2, pin

F. Coat

G. Belt

H. White full seat breeches

I. Beige full seat breeches

J. Dressage boots w/trees

K. Field boots w/trees

IX. Cross Country Attire

A. Helmet cover

B. Red polo shirt

C. Tipperary vest

D. Medical armband

E. Yellow watch

F. Red gloves

G. Navy breeches

X. Schooling Attire

A. Breeches

B. Purple helmet w/gloves

C. Polo boots

XI. Other clothes

A. Pajamas

B. T shirts

C. Sweatshirts

D. Vest

E. Coats

   1. CNDC jacket

   2. Goretex jackets

   3. Drizabone

   4. Kyra K coat

F. Skort

G. Shorts

H. Underwear

I. Bras

J. Socks

K. Footwear

    1. Barn boots

    2. Buck boots

    3. Non-barn shoes

L. Hats

    1. Rain

    2. Sun

    3. Baseball cap

M. Jeans

N. Non-horse clothes

O. Seasonal clothes:

    1. Polarfleece x 3

    2. Long johns

    3. Winter coat

XII. Personal

A. Traveling toiletry kit

    1. Makeup

    2. Hairdryer

B. Extra sunscreen

D. Sunglasses

E. Alarm clock

F. Water

G. Energy bars

H. Backpack

    1. Tylenol

    2. Arnica

    3. Maps, directions

    4. Omnibus, rulebook

    5. Tests

    6. Extra socks/underwear

    7. Video

I. Cooler

    1. Fruit

    2. Food

    3. Ice

J. Purse

    1. Wallet w/money

    2. Checkbook

    3. Cell phone + charger

K. Copies in glove box

    1. Truck registration

    2. Trailer registration

    3. Vehicle insurance

    4. Membership cards

    5. Coggins

OTHER SOURCES OF INFORMATION

READING

Reading is no substitute for experience or for the guidance of a qualified professional, but it is certainly the best enhancement you can find. I have books that I have read through when I first got them, but I keep them handy for reference at all times. Other books I use exclusively for reference, and still others I have read once and that was enough. The books that follow are on my "absolute must read" list (alphabetical by author). Find them and enjoy!

In addition to books, subscriptions to select magazines will round out your education and keep it current. Although there are other magazines I also enjoy, *The Chronicle of the Horse* and *Practical Horseman* are the ones I couldn't do without.

Bertalan de Nemethy

The De Nemethy Method. Bert de Nemethy was one of the most influential individuals in American show jumping, and this book describes his training techniques. Like Jimmy Wofford's book, this one includes ample ideas for gymnastics and courses.

Equine Research Library

Feeding to Win II. Most equine nutrition books are horribly confusing, but this one is quite readable and well laid out. Enjoy!

The Illustrated Veterinary Encyclopedia for Horsemen. Although the book is probably soon due for a revision, there is still plenty of sound, basic healthcare information. A useful reference.

German National Equestrian Federation

The Principles of Riding. The German FN's book clearly explains the theory and its application for training young horses and beginning riders correctly. It is also useful for reschooling horses, or simply for understanding the often overlooked basic principles which should govern our day-to-day training. This book and its companion, *Advanced Techniques of Riding*, are among my favorite and most frequently referred-to books.

Advanced Techniques of Riding. Building upon *The Principles of Riding*, this book explains the theory and practice of training at the highest levels of dressage, eventing, and show jumping. Both books are well illustrated.

Susan Harris

Grooming to Win. The bible of grooming.

USPC Manuals (D, C, B/HA/A), also by Susan Harris. Even if you've had horses for quite a while, you will find useful information on horse care and riding in all three levels of the manual. You can buy the manuals in many tack stores and mail order catalogs, or through USPC directly at 4071 Iron Works Parkway, Lexington, KY 40511-8462. www.pony-club.org. (606)254-7669.

USPC Guide: Conformation, Movement, and Soundness by Susan Harris. A concise and clear treatise on the above. For in-depth conformation and lameness reading, I like O. R. Adams, but for most purposes this book is all that is needed. As with all of Susan Harris' books, the illustrations are excellent.

Malcolm Kelley

The Stud Book. An illustrated guide for which studs to use under what conditions, and how to properly use them. Although not widely available, you can find this book at Dover Saddlery.

Virginia Leng

Training the Event Horse. For years Ginny Leng (now Elliot, previously Holgate) was one of the most successful event riders in Great Britain. This book gives you a glimpse of Ginny's program:

how they selected, managed, and trained horses from youngsters to the four star level.

Major Anders Lindgren

Major Anders Lindgren's Teaching Exercises. A well-thought-out collection of schooling exercises through the levels of dressage. Maj. Lindgren is truly one of the great masters of dressage, and in his book he clearly explains why you should do which exercise when and what you are trying to accomplish.

George Morris

Hunter Seat Equitation. The definitive book on how to ride in hunt seat by the man whose name is synonymous with equitation. Even if you are a jumper or event rider you will find useful information in this book. Plus, the section on teaching is excellent.

W. Müseler

Riding Logic. Müseler's classic text on training and retraining of the horse in dressage, cross country, and show jumping is highly readable and easy to understand and apply due to its systematicity. It is usually my first source when I am looking for clarification on a training issue.

Sally Swift

Centered Riding. I love this book. Somewhat akin to martial arts on horseback, it combines biomechanics with an artistic "right brained" approach to riding in a way that has helped many a rider overcome difficulties in position, balance, and suppleness as pertaining to a variety of disciplines. I particularly like the use of imagery.

United States Pony Clubs, Inc.

USPC Guide—Bandaging Your Horse. An excellent primer on all types of bandages. It is amazing how many people bandage their horses incorrectly, resulting in needless injuries and discomfort. Learn to do it right!

USPC Guide to Trailering. This booklet has a wealth of trailer maintenance, training, and safety information inside its unassuming stapled pages. Years after he first looked at it, my dad still loves to quote from this book.

James C. Wofford

Training the Three-Day Event Horse and Rider. Jimmy Wofford teaches or has taught nearly every USET three-day rider in the current era. If you want to learn how the big guns do it, read Jimmy's book. As a sidenote, all the photographs in the book are of Jimmy, his family, or his students, adding a personal touch to the work. There are also plenty of useful diagrams of gymnastics and courses at the back of the book.

SHOPPING!

Using this section as a resource, you should be able to find every product, piece of equipment, or item of apparel mentioned in this book, plus many more.

Mail Order Catalogs

I am a great fan of the local tack store. However, all of our needs can't always be met locally. If all the tack stores in your area focus, for example, on the region's hunter/jumper clientele and you event, you will need to look elsewhere. These are my favorite elsewheres, and they are why I have my credit card numbers committed to memory!

Bit of Britain

141 Union School Road
Oxford, PA 19363
www.bitofbritain.com
1-800-972-7985

If you event, you can find everything you need here. Everything I have bought from Bit of Britain is high quality, and John Nunn and his staff are knowledgeable and happy to help you figure out what you need. John also has a highly addictive website, www.tackoftheday.com, where he sells a different item at bargain basement prices every day. If you get on the email list you'll never miss a day!

Dover Saddlery
P.O. Box 1100
525 Great Road
Littleton, MA 01460
www.doversaddlery.com
1-800-989-1500   Fax: 508-429-8295

Dover has a large selection like State Line, but Dover's focus is more on serious competitive riders in the Olympic disciplines instead of State Line's broader focus. I find something that I need almost every time I pick up Dover's catalog...it's quite dangerous! They also have good prices, and even without special rush ordering, their shipping time of in-stock merchandise is usually outstanding.

Dressage Extensions
27501 Cumberland Road
Tehachapi, CA 93561
www.DressageExtensions.com
1-800-541-3708   Fax: 661-821-0317

Short of going to Europe, you will find one of the best selections of dressage equipment and apparel in this California-based catalog. There are also plenty of gift ideas.

Euro-American Saddlery
176 Highway 202
Ringoes, NJ 08551
www.eurosaddlery.com
1-888-SNAFFLE   Fax: 908-788-7690

I think of it as the East Coast's Dressage Extensions. Charlie and Romy Tota have a great selection at competitive prices. Between these two catalogs, you should be able to find all the dressage paraphernalia you need!

State Line Tack
1989 Transit Way
P.O. Box 935
Brockport, NY 14420-0935
www.statelinetack.com
1-800-228-9208   Fax: 716-637-1484

You can find a wide variety of horsecare, apparel, gift, and tack products at State Line. Their prices are generally the best, but some of the brands they carry aren't as high quality as others. If you buy tack, horse clothing, or apparel here, make sure it is a quality brand. State Line is usually my first choice for grooming and healthcare supplies due to their excellent prices.

Tack-in-the-Box
P.O. Box 158
Sublimity, OR 97385
www.tackinthebox.com
1-800-456-8225

Everything from this Oregon tack shop is useful and high quality. Connie Micheletti and her associates are helpful, knowledgeable horsepeople who are a pleasure to work with. The tack and apparel focus toward the dressage market, but there are other products with a broader appeal that are usually not found elsewhere.

Vet Supply Catalogs

KV Vet Supply
3190 North Road
P.O. Box 245
David City, NE 68632
www.kvvet.com
1-800-423-8211   Fax: 800-269-0093

They don't have the glossy pictures or informative descriptions of other catalogs, but if you know what you need, vet supply catalogs often give you far better prices than any other source. KV is a good one, as are Heartland and American Livestock.

American Livestock Supply, Inc.
P.O. Box 8441
Madison, WI 53708-8441
www.americanlivestock.com
1-800-356-0700   Fax: 800-309-8947

Heartland Vet Supply
5052 West 12th Street
Hastings, NE 68901
www.vetwarehouse.com
1-800-934-9398   Fax: 402-463-2115

Bargain Hunting

Riding is an expensive sport, and horses are costly to maintain. In terms of equipment, bargains are hard to find. You often save money in the long run by making a more expensive purchase at the outset and thereby avoid replacing items as frequently. However, there are a few ways to find better than average prices.

Internet: I have had luck with Herbie Rijndorp's www.equestquality.com, and I've known people who have bought happily from www.divoza.com. Both these online stores are based in

Europe where many items (particularly dressage and show jumping things) are less expensive, and even after paying shipping you can save substantially. The tricky part is the sizing: clothes run in European sizes; bits, stirrup leathers, etc. are measured in centimeters and millimeters instead of inches. Make sure you know exactly what size you need before ordering. The same goes if you buy from eBay—you can get some amazing deals, but know your size in the brand you're bidding on. Also check out John Nunn's www.tackoftheday.com; there is a great new item every day at an unbelievable price!

Sales: Many tack stores will have sales of season-specific items at the end of that season, and if you have the foresight to buy that winter turnout rug in April and hang onto it till the following November, you can save a bit. If you happen to wear a funky size, so much the better. When I was eleven, I bought my first pair of tall boots on sale for about one-tenth the retail price because they were not a commonly sought-after size. Also, sometimes things are mislabeled size-wise, which may keep them on the shelf long enough that they end up on sale. A barn jacket in size "large" that is labeled "small" will get tried on by people looking for a small, and it won't fit them. So if you see something you want and it says it's the wrong size, try it out before writing it off.

Tack swaps: Many local equestrian organizations, USDF GMO's (group member organizations), and Pony Clubs will periodically hold tack swaps. Depending on the scope and type of equipment sold, you can often find some useful stuff. I think of eBay as a virtual tack swap!

Supermarkets, craft stores, and drugstores: You will probably be able to get Murphy's Oil Soap, castile soap, boot polish, yarn, needles, etc. cheaper here than you would at a tack store. But avoid buying shoe polishing supplies at your shoe repair guy's shop, unless you can't find them anywhere else: usually the quantities will be smaller and the prices higher than either a tack store or a supermarket/drugstore.

Automotive supply store: Hands down the best place to buy rags for tack cleaning, boot polishing, and horse shining. If you need to clean rubber for any reason, you can also buy your Armorall Tuff Stuff here.

ABOUT THE AUTHOR

Jennifer Chong grew up in Cupertino, California, doing hunter/jumpers, eventing, dressage, trail riding, hunting and mounted games in the heart of Silicon Valley. She has been a working student at eventing and dressage barns across the United States and in Germany. Jennifer is an HA rated Pony Club graduate from Pacific Ridge Pony Club. In 2000, she graduated from the University of California, Davis, with a degree in psychology and concentrations in linguistics and Spanish. While at UC Davis, Jennifer rode briefly on the school's intercollegiate hunt seat equitation team before taking a friend's horse to regional and national awards at preliminary level eventing and second level dressage.

After spending two years in Maryland, Jennifer moved to Massachusetts to study at Harvard Law School. She graduated with a juris doctor degree in 2005. Jennifer, her dog, cat and horse now live in San Diego.

For an ongoing forum of helpful hints and ideas for turnout, go to www.tothenines.org.

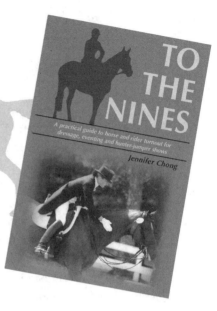

If you liked

TO THE NINES

you will also enjoy . . .

How to Use Leg Wraps, Bandages and Boots
by Sue Allen

A handy guide to sizing and fitting boots, applying polo and standing

wraps, heat and cold therapy and more.
Softcover, $17.95
ISBN 0-931866-72-3

The Equine Arena Handbook
by Robert Malmgren

Arena footing, drainage and maintenance are vital considerations for dressage or jumping. Before you build or renovate

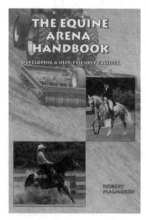

an arena, read this book. It will pay off by preventing injury and facilitating top performance.
Softcover, $17.95
ISBN 1-57779-016-2

Helping People Succeed with Horses and Dogs
For a current listing of book titles, visit us at:
www.alpinepub.com